LOV
YOU
MUM

LOVE
YOU
MUM

Stop Trying to be the Mum
You Think You Should Be

Start Enjoying Being
the Mum You Are

GILLIAN CAMPBELL

First published by Barnes Holland Publishing Ltd in 2011

Barnes Holland Publishing Ltd
The Old Star
Church Street
Princes Risborough
HP27 9AA

ISBN: 978-0-9563128-1-5

British Library Cataloguing in Publication Data
A catalogue record for this book is available from the
British Library.

Illustrations by Alan Hayball (http://ahayball.co.uk), based
on ideas by Emma Burgess (www.freakypigeon.com).

Cover photo by Amberword Photography.

Printed in the UK.

CONTENTS

CONTENTS

LOVE YOU MUM

It's not only children who grow. Parents do too. As much as we watch to see what our children do with their lives, they are watching us to see what we do with ours. I can't tell my children to reach for the sun. All I can do is reach for it, myself. —**Joyce Maynard**

This is a self-development book, but let's be clear from the start: it's not a beat-yourself-about-the-head-because-you're-not-good-enough book, or an another-tick-in-the-"I'm-a-failure"-box book, or a self-righteous list of essential disciplines to achieve an impossible level of perfection that Super Mum herself would fail to aspire to. It is a book with a collection of ideas and learning that I and other mums have at times found useful, sometimes crucial, funny and thought provoking. It will at times be a sanity check, a challenge or an emotional journey. First and foremost, it is written with an intention to bring you ways to feel more resourceful, content and accepting, not more disappointed, frustrated or useless.

This book is written for you, a mum who adores your children and embraces the life they bring you. Yet through your child-led, hectic, busy days, you may find yourself occasionally having a vague inkling that you left behind or lost a part of yourself when you had children. Perhaps there is a nagging feeling about the absence of a part of yourself which you haven't yet fully rediscovered. You love your children, you would not change having had them, and yet it could be at times you are not fully living life in the way you would like to – at the very least, it seems like life is living you.

1

Whereas some of you may never feel ahead of or even equal to your day-to-day work and tasks, others may end the day wishing they had been gentler and more patient with their children, more productive in what they did and more loving and understanding with their partner and themselves. Maybe you wish you'd laughed, smiled and embraced challenges more than you shouted, moaned or got stressed. Some mums would love to stop feeling an unacknowledged, underlying resentment about the constant juggling to meet others' wants and needs, to stop battling against a level of strain that seems slowly to eat away at their mood. In addition, you would like to turn off the voices in your head that worry about guilt or "What will they think?" and hearing the harshest critic of all, your own inner voice, replacing them with acceptance and understanding.

Or maybe life as a mum is not this bleak for you. You may have already passed the first few years of your children's lives and now be ready to start thinking clearly about yourself again. Maybe your children have grown up and moved away and you are wondering what is next. Or for you the early years of your children's lives may be the happiest, most fulfilled you have ever been and you are wondering how to keep that level of fulfilment as your children move on to school. The examples in the book are predominantly about new mums with extreme challenges, but don't let that cloud your view of the work. I have 100% positive feedback that every mum and grandmum with children of all ages has found exercises that have helped them become more of the mum, the woman, they want to be.

If you have the desire to embrace motherhood, not based on a dream of being a perfect yummy mummy or alpha mum or the illusion of having it all, but from a foundation of honest, transparent joy at being the fulfilled and

2

satisfied woman you are, with all your strengths and challenges, then this is the book for you. So read on...

When you have children you are in a role with no job description, no performance review or appraisal, no structured business planning or goal setting, no constructive impartial feedback, no training courses and no pay rise or bonuses. Particularly if you've had all those elements in your working life, you may be bewildered and lost, with no idea of how well you're doing.

This book puts some structure and clarity around the multifaceted role of being a mum. It will clarify your expectations about yourself and help you to accept or change who you are and how you feel about yourself as a mum. The book leads you through a journey of discovery or rediscovery, to a you who is more at peace with life as a mum.

It looks at the expectations of those around you, both the youngest members of your family and your partner, parents, friends, employers and work colleagues. It acknowledges the roots of some of the unresourceful feelings you may be having and shows you how to change either the way you think or the causes of the thoughts. By introducing or reminding you of some simple self-development techniques and methods of using your emotional intelligence, it will help you evaluate your hopes, goals and expectations as a mum.

The book doesn't contain any parenting techniques or tips, any tricks to get your children to sleep, eat or learn any differently than you are already doing. This book is for one of the most important influences on your children's life – you.

If you can't imagine making time to read a book purely for yourself, let alone starting to implement changes to make yourself happier, think about this:

Your children become what they see in you.

Changing the way you think, respond and grow in your life is the greatest way to show your children how they can too.

This book will not bring you inner peace, a shield of tranquil wisdom or a perfect life. What it will bring you is the realisation that you have a choice about how you live as a mum.

More days will end with you smiling and at ease with what you faced and actually enjoyed. Your relationships with all the people who mean the most to you will be more relaxed and more resourceful. You will find areas of joy, laughter and childlike silliness in your day-to-day life and you will transfer them to your children and loved ones. As you let go of your burdens and baggage, you will quite simply become lighter, brighter and more balanced.

Sometimes I will challenge you, ask you to look at yourself and honestly answer questions about the choices you are making. At other times the book will make you laugh at, question, reassess or support your hopes and fears. It will also stop you feeling alone with the doubts and fears that we all have as mums.

WORK IS EASIER!

In a working environment, a significant aspect of a person's worth comes from achievement and completion of a task. There is normally an end point and an outcome, then perhaps you move forward to a bigger and better challenge. You set a goal that is finite and you seek to find achievable outcomes that can be measured. On completion of a task there is often positive feedback, thanks and maybe even a reward. Obviously there are frustrations, clashes of personality, technical breakdowns and dead ends, but in essence there is a clear definition of achievement, success and failure. You have some choice over the outcomes and if everything goes wrong you have the ability to change job, career, direction and, worst-case scenario, just walk away.

From day one as a mum, when you give birth or become a mum to a child born to someone else, everything changes. From that moment forward, you are at least partly responsible for the wellbeing of another person. Your child or children at first rely totally on you and go on to require your love, guidance, energy and time, for the rest of their lives. You embark on the biggest "to-do" list of your life, never really being able to tick off many tasks, and even when you do, ten more appear.

The feedback and sense of achievement can be awesome when your child achieves a goal, be it smiling, talking, walking or winning a race, an academic achievement, a happy relationship or even parenthood for him- or herself. The joys, the pleasures and the highs almost always outweigh the negatives. Yet very often in reality there is little or no constructive, structured feedback of any kind and lots of, often conflicting, views and opinions about what you should or could have done.

By the working world's definitions, first and foremost motherhood is for ever. It has no universal definitions, no job description and no performance appraisal. Day to day there is no impartial feedback, no promotion, no pay rises, no lunch breaks, at times not even a pee break, on your own anyway! It often consists of many repetitive, thankless tasks combined with massive, life-changing decisions. It means making choices that can never really be quantified as correct, and yet every one has an effect on the life of your child.

Of course, there are not many jobs where a toothy grin, a soggy hug, uncontrollable giggles on a sunny day, a sleepy face at the end of a trip or a flower picked for you from the garden can bring such delight and satisfaction. But by seeing the role of a mum from the perspective of a workplace, it becomes clear why we can feel so overwhelmed and power-less at times.

AM I THE ONLY MUM WHO...?

Before writing this book I started an online forum called "Am I am the only Mum who...?" at www.theonlymum.com. This is a safe place where we can start being totally honest about the benefits and the joys but also the fears, doubts, pain and sometimes dislikes of being a mum. I quickly realised that a perfectly content, perfectly calm mum was just a myth – everyone at times finds being a mum a chal-lenge in one way or another. From this platform I decided to start letting other mums know that sometimes we all find it hard and that not only does that not make us a bad mum, in fact it makes us a stronger, braver, more honest mum as we stop trying to live a myth and live as we are, mistakes, doubts, fears, dreams, passions, strengths and all.

Mothers around the world come in many different shapes and sizes, with many different characteristics, atti-tudes, beliefs and cultures. Some of us become mothers by carrying our children within us and giving birth to them, some of us through other ways. All of us share one funda-mental goal: we are charged with human souls who look to us for their safety, their security, their strength and as a source of love.

We may choose to be with our children full time, or we may choose to work for our own mental growth or because we have to. We may be apart from our children through our own choice or against our will. We may have a partner, a network of friends, family members, a religion. We may be facing the joys and challenges of supporting and guiding our children through life's joys and pain on our own. At times it may feel an awesome privilege, and sometimes a heavy burden. But one thing has become very clear to me. There is always another mum somewhere who has experienced what you are feeling right now, and there is always another mum who can bring solace, support, levity and encouragement when you need it.

Love You Mum is for every mum – working, full time, part time, single, married, adoptive, step, foster and every other variety. Its aim is to help us stop feeling we are different in a negative way and start embracing our differences for all the positives they bring. As you read through the book, some of the examples may not seem relevant to the mum you are. I often use the circumstances of brilliant mums when they were most challenged, to show how the learning can work at the worst of times. For you they may just enhance the best of times. Observe them with curiosity, share the challenges other mums are facing and store anything you learn in case you or another fellow mum could use it another day.

THE JOURNEY TO A TRUTH

In my working life before I had children, I trained senior executives, directors and CEOs in how to use emotional intelligence to realise their personal potential. I encouraged an awareness of their inner state and a level of analysis of how their bodies and minds were feeling and performing, adjusting to circumstances as they happened. I advocated simple mindset techniques to help them make choices that brought success and confidence, a sense of personal achievement and happiness with the choices that they made. I concentrated on the ability to manage their own emotions while being aware of and empathic to the emotions of others.

The process I designed to do this is called:

A TRUTH

It is a journey through the following steps:

Awareness
Thoughts
Reality
Understanding
Take response-ability
Habits

What I realised when I became a mum, particularly after I had my second child, is that A TRUTH is not only a workplace tool for executives, it is essential for my sanity as a mum. It is the basis for this book and it underpins the journey I want you to take with me.

Awareness
First we look at raising our self-awareness, becoming aware of our inner critic, and turning off guilt, self-criticism and self-doubt and the stress they create.

Thoughts
Secondly, we examine the impact our thoughts have on our behaviour. We identify the needs that lie beneath our thoughts and the feelings that grow from them. We learn how we can meet our own needs and balance them with the needs of others. We also examine how our thoughts are created from stories that are often not based on the truth, but on the assumptions that we have created.

*R*eality

I will share with you a method of accepting the reality of every situation you find yourself in as a mum. I show how you can reduce your stress and suffering even when events seem unmanageable.

*U*nderstanding

I explain how you can start to understand why you feel the way you do, and how to accept and understand who and where you are now.

*T*ake response-ability

Not a recurring typo, this is about increasing your ability to respond resourcefully. I help you to find a surefire way, in every circumstance, to choose your response and improve your response-ability. You will take full response-ability for setting a future for yourself as a mum and how you meet the needs of the woman inside you.

*H*abits

I help you find the method that will work for you to create new goals and habits and to stick to them.

I am not a professor of psychology, and the theory behind these techniques is not exclusively my own or even unique. I combine self-help and top executive coaching techniques, simple life planning, my experience and that of the mums I have talked to in a process that will help you find clarity in your thinking and a structure for your future plans. As I said, the examples through the book often take the darkest, more challenging elements of mums' experiences. If you have never felt as bleak as the mums I discuss, if their challenge does not apply to you, don't turn off and feel that the learning doesn't apply. Read on and utilise the learning, as many, many confident and happy mums have still gained much from these practices. This book explores a set of ideas and skills that, when life's challenges are overwhelming or just plain relentless, bring you a choice about how you handle your life as a mum and a woman. It is an opportunity for you to be able to look yourself in the mirror and say to yourself: "I love you mum."

See reading the book as "me time", a well-deserved sanctuary for you and you alone to re-evaluate, think, plan and achieve a greater sense of self-worth, purpose and success.

On a practical point, as I know there's nothing worse than starting something only to find you don't have everything you need to complete it, while you read through the book you will need something to write with and something to write in and keep to hand.

Also in the book are exercises to complete and to provoke reflection and analysis. Some of the exercises are fun and frivolous, some will touch you in positive ways, some will challenge you. Of course, it is entirely your choice whether you complete the exercises, but my suggestion is to treat them as you would a quiz in a magazine, with intrigue and a sense of curiosity. Complete only one at a time and try not to get bogged down into too many in one sitting. They are as much part of your journey as any techniques or skills you will learn from the book.

If life is busy and you would love to read this book but right now don't have a hope of finding the time, at the end of every chapter there is a summary called Mindset in a Minute, a quick recap of the key practical points from each stage of the journey. You could use those to focus in on the area you feel is most important for you at the moment.

MY STORY

In my teenage years I had a plan: I would have a successful career, fall in love, have babies, give up work and be an amazing mum. I would nurture and guide my children's first few years, then rekindle my working life and effortlessly and brilliantly combine family and work.

Subsequent challenges became an eventful time finding Mr Right and a journey of discovery about fertility. Suffice to say I am eternally grateful and appreciative to have been able to have children at all.

Yet there I was at 40, my 2 year old in the middle of potty training and all the exquisite joy and body fluids that brings, my 5 month old still waking every two hours through the night for breastfeeding, screaming himself to sleep, screaming for food and in fact screaming for most things (chronic reflux – poor chap!).

My husband was away in London all week to pay our bills, leaving me alone on a permanent 24-hour shift. I had switched a company car for an old people carrier that was permanently covered in a random selection of unidentified stains, with a heady odour of stale milk and vomit. I had swapped an executive to-do list for a fifth load of washing, a trip to the supermarket with my calculator and coupons and researching how to get felt tip out of carpets. I had continual illnesses and couldn't remember the last time I'd had five minutes to myself, let alone with my husband. I went back to work and nothing became easier, there was just more of it – although to be truthful I did get the chance to pee, eat a sandwich and get a coffee on my own and the freedom of gaining achievement outside of my home.

It was hard for me to admit, but at times I felt frustrated, disempowered and exhausted with motherhood. Added to this joyful state, somewhere along the line I stopped being a person and started introducing myself at the rare social gathering as either Josh or Jake's mum or, a catch-all for me, "Just a mum".

When did I lose my connection to my old self, my joy, my pride and my excitement? I found myself berating my beautiful baby for crying, snapping at my elder son for the slightest thing and feeling resentful and exploding regularly at my husband, blaming him and him alone for the woes of the world. I was still pulling on shapeless maternity clothes and rarely bothering with make-up, let alone shaving my legs or moisturising my parched, sleep-deprived skin.

I was aware from the media that the average working mum works an 18-hour day. This is the same media that show me a blissfully glowing footballer's wife with her 6-week-old baby in her size zero arms. Society today pro-motes supermums, alpha-mums, yummy mummies and those who run businesses from home and still manage to make jam and homemade cakes for their children. That was a long way from my reality. Was I such a failure? Was I the only mum?

I quickly became aware that it wasn't only me who was vulnerable to this idea of being just a mum. Other women felt many similar things, on a spectrum of everything from being devalued, frustrated, overwhelmed and worn down, to incompetent and lacking as mums and most importantly as women. We may have felt like we are doing OK, achieving our best, but we always wanted to grow and feel as if we were developing as mums. We were tasked with the role of creating the next generation, nourishing, enriching and inspiring beautiful young souls, and yet we were working from a personal baseline with many challenges, either from of a lack of self-worth, low energy and withering self-confidence, or just a level of uncertainty as to how well we were doing.

We cannot yet change the media's view of motherhood or society's attitudes to mothering and we cannot fight decades of belief that a mother's needs should come last. What we can change, one mum at a time, is what we feel about *ourselves*.

We can make our lives quieter, increase our peace of mind, lower our stress levels and find a place of acceptance, calm and stillness, a haven from the frantic world around us. We can simply improve on where we are now by adding some new personal development tools to our armoury and feeling like we are doing something purely for ourselves. Life as a mum can become easier not by changing your children, partner, job or environment, but by changing the way you feel about them and about *you*.

MINDSET IN A MINUTE
LOVE YOU MUM...

Am I the only mum who...
...feels overwhelmed, confused, exhausted, spent, burnt out, selfish, elated, satisfied, complete, replete, confident, relaxed, calm?

Never, there are many of us who feel exactly the same. You are not the only mum. Stop living in a myth of what you believe you should be – start living as the woman, the mum, you are.

In comparison to any remunerated role, motherhood comes with no job description, no performance review, no appraisal, no business plan, no pay rise, no constructive feedback, no weekend or holidays. So don't be surprised that you're not always sure if you're doing a good job!

Love You Mum will help you find clarity and acceptance of how you see the role of mum for you. You will start to examine your own and others' subconscious expectations and the standards you are measured against as a mum. You will gain a clearer understanding of your own measures of failure and success and why you feel dissatisfied as a result.

Now is the time to truly look at yourself and start to accept or build changes.

Your children become what they see in you!

Love You Mum follows the journey through A TRUTH:

♡ **A**wareness – Start to know who you are and whether you are happy with her.
♡ **T**houghts – Look at the impact of your thoughts on your behaviour towards others and yourself.
♡ **R**eality – Start to be truthful with yourself and accept the reality of where you are and why you are there.
♡ **U**nderstanding – Start to forgive, accept and gain a clear picture of what you would like to change.
♡ **T**ake response-ability – Start taking charge of your choices, your future, your life.
♡ **H**abits – Build the habits you need to live your life as you want it to be.

CHAPTER 1

BECOMING AWARE

When you are looking in the mirror, you are looking at the problem. But, remember, you are also looking at the solution. **—Anon**

Self-awareness is the first step on any journey to rediscover or redefine who we are after big changes have happened in our lives – and becoming a mum is one of the biggest.

Self-awareness is the process of looking at yourself and discovering why you feel like you do and do the things you do. The aim is to create the ultimate freedom of being able to accept who you are, your strengths and weaknesses, and to choose your actions, behaviour and responses to any situation.

No one else can become a greater expert on you than *you*. No one else can listen, learn and grow to know you the way you can. When you're clear about who you are, what you need and why you need it, you're empowered to consciously and actively make your needs, goals and dreams a reality.

WHY IS BECOMING AWARE IMPORTANT?

There are two aspects to the everyday – even 24-hour – stresses that mums face. There are the events themselves: tummy bugs, tantrums, washing machines and cars breaking down, traffic jams after school drop-off on the way to work, missed deadlines and childcare challenges. Things like these are inevitable. They will happen day in day out, and in essence you have limited control over them.

The second element is the mood these events throw you into: the snapping at your children, the resentment and moaning at your partner, the bitching and grumbling with your friends, the low mood and disappointment at another grumpy day, the anger and frustration. It maybe that you do manage to keep up a positive front for your children, yet when they are in bed you have nothing left for you or your partner.

Becoming self-aware passes the ownership and the responsibility for your mood, your frustrations and your anger right back to you. The path of A TRUTH and its exercises and mindset techniques will explain how you can choose how you handle, respond to and control the way you act following these events. You will be able to navigate through your days consciously choosing how you think, feel and behave rather than just reacting and potentially being disappointed in your actions.

When you are self-aware you will be able to sit down at the end of the day, knots gone from your stomach, a smile on your face and a glass of wine in your hand that you fancy but don't need! But it also means that you will no longer be able to blame your kids, husband, mother-in-law, boss, hormones, tiredness or any other factor for how you feel about yourself.

You and only you can learn how to be at peace with your life and yourself. If at the moment you don't feel you're ready to let go of your excuses, either put the book down, or hold your scepticism close and see if by the end you agree with me.

MEET YOUR BIGGEST CRITIC AND BIGGEST FAN

The other reason becoming self-aware is essential, particularly as a mum, is that it allows you to meet head-on your biggest critic, the tallest hurdle to you breaking free from self-limiting beliefs. This is the voice of your guilt, self-doubt, regret, stress and fear. It is your inner voice.

"I don't have one of those, Gill!"

Who said that?

You did, or your inner voice did.

Let me ask it a question: "Are you happy right now?"

Did you hear the answer?

Your inner voice knows how you feel about yourself. Throughout this book I will be asking you to listen to it very carefully, both when it speaks from its place as your critic and when it speaks as your fan. Learn to listen to it, understand what it's saying and when necessary master and control it and it will become a source of power, enabling you to overcome challenges and where necessary make peace with situations that are beyond your control. When you do, you will come to know that you are living as you want to.

Trust me, your inner voice can help you if you will only take the time and have the patience and self-awareness to listen.

This book is a journey, and before you plan your journey, you need to be fully aware of where you are starting from.

The first step is for you to work out what your personal starting point is on your journey to being the mum you want to be, or being OK with being the mum you are. This is where I ask you to start working with me, to look inside yourself.

If you have an underlying, nagging sense of dissatisfaction with yourself or your life, you need to analyse where

19

that's coming from. In the workplace, to find a solution to a problem we first analyse what the cause, contributions and component parts of the problem are. This is situational analysis, thinking briefly about a desired state, looking at your current state and establishing the gap between the two. Unlike most work situations, when you are looking at your own mindset, you can't always apply logic to your thoughts and feelings. You will be listening purely to your intuition from your inner voice.

I'm asking you to talk to yourself!

TUNE IN TO YOUR INNER VOICE

Throughout the book I will be asking you to discover from your inner voice your opinions and thoughts on different areas of your journey into your life as a mum, through exercises and questions for reflection.

Question, interrogate and analyse your thoughts. Think about whether they may be society's, the media, your parents', your employer's and friends' views, or whether they are in fact your own opinion and truly from your inner voice.

If you have followed a path of personal development in your life so far this will be a process you will be used to and hopefully embrace (although you may not have previously applied your own personal developmental learning to the context or role of being a mum). For some of you, though, this may be one of the first times you have stopped to think about and analyse your thoughts, so it may feel self-indulgent, scary or just plain weird.

In my years of experience working with people to reach their full potential and grow to accept who they are, I have become convinced that any time spent analysing your thoughts, feeling and opinions is time getting to know yourself. That knowledge can bring understanding, acceptance and often an awareness of the path to change.

The very fact that you are reading this book means that some part of you is ready to do this. Another lesson that years of leading and helping develop people have taught me is that if something feels awkward, uncomfortable or scary, it is more than likely relevant and useful for you.

The box contains a few words of guidance for making best use of the exercises in this book.

MAKING BEST USE OF THE AWARENESS EXERCISES

♡ Make time. Flip through each chapter before you start it to find out how many periods of reflection, questioning or thinking there are (they'll be in a box like this so they're easy to spot). Either read through the chapter and do the exercises later, or only begin the chapters knowing you have given yourself enough time. Giving yourself time as a mum is sometimes almost impossible, I know. There are always tasks and demands on your time, be they in the house, workplace, children or relationships. However, my very strong belief is that you will tackle and embrace those tasks with greater clarity, motivation and joy if you have also taken time to meet some of your own needs and listened to your inner voice first.

♡ Find somewhere quiet, but not so quiet you could fall asleep (or is that only me?).

♡ Make yourself a space both physically and mentally where there will be minimal interruptions and grab yourself a drink, preferably non-alcoholic; our inner voice gets drunk just as quickly as we do!

♡ Have something to write with and a book to write your thoughts down in. I am a great believer in using a journal or workbook to recount your entire journey. If you don't have such a book, a piece of paper will suffice – it's the mental process that counts, not a faultless, grammatically correct written account. (Plus if you are prone to procrastination, a trip to the shops for stationery is a lovely day's diversion, but not why you bought this book!)

♡ In each exercise, ask yourself the question and then just sit and listen or watch what your mind does with it.

♡ Some people find it useful to note down thoughts as they appear. As you write one word other relevant linked words may arise for you, so write them all down as they come. When the thought stream has quietened, rank or rate the thoughts as to how important they feel to you.

♡ Or you may prefer just to observe, listen to the thoughts that flow from the question, sit and hear them without judgement or analysis and wait for your mind to settle on a final viewpoint.

♡ It isn't important initially to clarify how these thoughts or voice were formed, whether they come from childhood, society or the media, for example. Just be aware of how they resonate with you.

♡ Finally, do write down the key words that answer the question the exercise has posed to your mind.

♡ As you progress through the book you will find the method that is useful to you and the one you feel most comfortable with.

WHAT KIND OF MUM DO YOU WANT TO BE?

Each of us may see success as a mum and a woman in very different terms. The words I hear when working with mums vary tremendously:

From many I hear: "When my children are happy, I'm happy, I feel I've done a good job for that day!" Some people rate themselves by their children's visible results, academic, sporting or financial; some by their children's personal milestones. Others rate themselves by their own achievements, either looking smart and attractive every day and having a beautiful house, or achieving career goals, breakthrough achievements in their chosen field, and showing role-model behaviour to their children.

For some, having their life back to a similar place to where they were before they had children represents success; for others, a life revolving around their offspring is totally desirable.

Some base their ideal on what they learned from watching their own mum bring them and their siblings up and choose either the same path or the exact opposite. Others have a vision pictured many years ago, maybe even in childhood, of what "Mummy" looks like. For some, what they deem as appropriate and acceptable as a mum comes from the influence of literature, their employer, media or culture.

For many, me included, just having more smiles than tears and more laughter than shouting is a great place to be, or an occasional moment of calm or shared contentment as I settle my boys to sleep.

Each of these is a personal measure of success. If it feels like success, embrace it – mums deserve all the good feelings they can grab!

One thing I can guarantee is that, given time to think and reflect, we can all describe what a good mum looks like to us, what psychologists call the "desired state".

EXERCISE 1
WHAT IS YOUR CURRENT (UNCONSCIOUS) VIEW OF
WHAT A GOOD MUM LOOKS LIKE?

These questions may seem very open to interpretation and ambiguous and of course they are, they are designed to get your personal reaction. There is no right answer and no points awarded, you just need to decide the starting point of your views on being a mum, right now. This is a gentle, simple step into your inner thoughts; we will go much deeper later in the book.

Was your mum a good mum?
If yes, why?
If no, why?
If you don't know, why?

Before becoming a mum, how would you have described what a good mum was like?
What did you think made a bad mum?

Having become a mum, what do you now believe makes a bad mum?

Having become a mum, what do you now believe makes a good mum?

What character traits does she have?

How does a good mum feel about herself?

Are there times that you feel any of these things about yourself?

Finally, what would your children say makes a good mum (even if they can't talk yet)?

How many of the things they would say would you like to make part of you?

Do you do that?

This exercise highlights your inner vision of being a mum, your dream or idealised characterisation of what being a great or poor mum looks like to you. Were you aware of these opinions or this picture before you answered the questions?

It will also have shown you your initial feelings about how close to that vision you are. This is a starting point for exploring where some of your dissatisfaction may lie – or maybe a wonderful illustration of how well you are actually doing by your own calibration.

Steven Covey, a very successful proponent of achieving personal potential, advocates in his book *The 7 Habits of Highly Effective People*® that to begin a journey of self-discovery we should begin with the end in mind. In this case, you're beginning with what you currently perceive to be the desired state, the ideal mum.

This vision you have initially captured will for now be set as your desired state. I will ask you to remain aware of this and reflect on how your opinions of it may alter as you work through the book.

WHO ARE YOU?

OK, let's cut to the quick. Before we go any further, we need to talk honestly and share a few home truths. Being a mum looks very different to each one of us. You will be where you are due to choice, circumstance, chance or sheer coincidence, but whichever it is you will have a view of other mums. Here are a few views of mums that I would like to introduce you to, and some myths that you may or may not associate with each.

MUMMY MYTHS

First we have the *full-time mum*, the mum who gets to focus solely on her children and relax and enjoy her home, creating wonderful, healthy meals, a spotless, harmonious house and calm, happy, well-rounded and stimulated children. She has the emotional security that she is doing the "right" thing for her children, giving them the best start and embodying the sanctity of true motherhood. She can put her children first and enjoy seeing every new experience they face, being beside them every step of the way.

Alternatively, she's the one who never gets to escape... ever! Her only feedback or input is from her children or partner when they can't find their pants, or something similarly catastrophic has happened. She's the mum who gets to do very little purely for herself. At times she may find her life repetitive, fruitless and a bit of a trap – she does believe that this is what she *should* be doing, but occasionally wishes it wasn't what she *is* doing! Added to that, now she's done that for five years and started her youngest at school, she panics about what to do next and is actually contemplating starting all over again with another child just to avoid having to do anything new.

Secondly there's the mum who has to work for money, who did not want to work and does not want a career – the *works-for-money mum*. This mum has a job she can walk away from at the end of the working day, forgetting her tasks and fully focusing on home when she is home, getting the best of both worlds: time off from home, time to catch up with colleagues and have adult conversations, and no pressure to grow, outperform and compete in the workplace. She feels she is contributing financially and gaining a sense of pride from that.

Or is that the mum who *has* to work, often with random hours, on top of being a mum, has no job satisfaction, no stimulation, no motivation to go to work, who faces tedium at work and then more tedium from housework at home. She feels she lets her children down with the hours she is away but has no satisfaction from either life. Her partner does not see her job as relevant or important, or at least not as important as his, and therefore sees no need to help more at home. If God forbid one of the children is ill and can't go to school, he'd never expect to stay at home with them.

Thirdly, we have the mum who chooses to work, the *loves-to-work mum*. She loves the challenge, the mental stimulation and the satisfaction of performing the role that she has often studied and trained to do. She loves her career not more than but differently to her children, but is happier with it than without; it keeps her sane. She believes that she is a better person, role model, woman and mum because she is living a life she loves and her children get the best of her passion for life and never miss out.

And yet she finds that she can't bring herself to tell everyone that. She knows that some people are disapproving: the sarky comments, the knowing looks, the headlines in the paper on the clinical trials showing that her children will apparently develop more slowly and be damaged by her choices. She is the one who is sat working before her children get up and after they go to bed. Who has to keep switching her mind to the children when she's with them as it keeps wandering to her work to-do list and who still worries about her children when she's at work. Who seems to be dropping balls in both roles and not achieving what she would like in either. Who gets home from a nine-hour day at the office to dive straight into bedtime with her children, then straight back into work once they're asleep. And who acknowledges that by not attending the departmental get-together at the wine bar, where much of the real business takes place, she will be stuck in catch-up mode the next day.

There is also the happily-married-and-supported mum myth that I hear from single mums and the amazing-freedom-of-parental-choice myth I get from partnered parents about single mums. The mums with able-bodied children, and those without. The mums who have religious expectations and support or pressure, and those who don't. The sandwich mum generation who not only parent and care for their children but also for their own parents or parents-in-law, and the mum who expends every ounce of who she is on everyone else.

Of course these are stereotypes, boxes, labels and judgements about the choices mums make. The varieties of mum are endless and this book is for each and every one of them, as equals, without judgement. Each mum will have chosen or fallen into her particular path, and once there may be satisfied or not. The key is that each of you now establishes whether the mum "box" you are in is where you want to be.

Each of these mummy myths embodies a part of the mum you are. Throughout the book you will hear examples from many different individual mums. In becoming aware you need to ask yourself which of those mums share characteristics with you, or write a description of yourself all of your own. When you have a picture of the mum you are, just ask yourself if that is what you originally wanted. Now you are living that picture, is it still the one you want?

WHAT IS STOPPING YOU?

With awareness comes a journey of investigation into all the influences and behaviours that have brought you to where you are now. I haven't met you, and through the medium of this book I obviously can't talk you through what your life has handed you to face. What I can do is share with you

WHAT KIND OF MUM DO YOU WANT TO BE ?

a list of the most common hurdles we face as mums, from talking to other mums and because I am one myself. These are our examples, and I will ask you to mentally calibrate how closely these scenarios fit the way you act or feel day to day as a mum.

If you do have other challenges that I don't cover, please feel free to share them confidentially on my website www.theonlymum.com, as I guarantee you there will be many other mums who feel exactly the same as you.

So, you have a created a perceived desired state or end point to your journey and you have asked yourself the first question about where you are on that journey. I'm now going to ask you to look at your present state and what the current barriers are to you achieving your desired end point.

Very simply put, you are born with your full potential. Throughout life you encounter experiences and role models, some of them useful and empowering, others limiting and disempowering. Those that fall into the latter category can generate inter-fear-ances that grow within you and act as a brake or even a total block to you achieving your desired performance. (For all you avid grammar spotters, this isn't a typo, it's the introduction into the concept that it is in part fear that is interfering with you reaching your potential.)

Potential – inter-fear-ance = performance

When I taught aerobics, I had to have a tough discussion with many 5 ft large-boned women that being a 6 ft size 6 supermodel was not a fair goal to aim for (a discussion I seem to keep having with myself recently about my own two-baby, lots-of-chocolate-and-crisps-affected body). But whatever the physical barriers, I believe that emotionally we all have the innate ability to be the person we strive to be.

We all can choose how we respond mentally, we have the potential to perform to and achieve our desired outcome. What prevents us from achieving this state is the build-up of inter-fear-ances.

You may as well start with the truth as you always end up with the truth. —**Earl Shoaf**

EXERCISE 2
WHAT IS STOPPING YOU DAY TO DAY?

Hear the other mums' voices below and see how they resonate with you. Then, using the summaries at the end of each section, analyse and score yourself from 1 to 10, with 10 being a high resemblance to your current state and 1 being not relevant at all. Be honest with yourself – you have nothing to gain by ignoring where you are and awareness brings clarity.

1. I used to be able to but I can't do that now.

I heard myself as a full-time mum with both kids at school, saying to my husband: "Can't you phone the insurance company from the office about the new quote, I just won't have time?"

Three weeks back to work after maternity leave I am asked to head up a brand new project, I knew it was the chance I had been waiting for but was absolutely terrified... Having worked in sales all my life, I was suddenly at a newly started evening class, entering a room full of people I had never met and finding it terrifying and stressful.

I realised that a day where I needed to pick up dry cleaning, get a prescription, do the supermarket shopping and return library books around the school runs seems like an awfully busy day.

Anything new, be it researching a new computer for my daughter or an energy provider for my house, had become a major task and really rather overwhelming.

♡ Compared to your life before you had children, have new situations or lists of tasks become stressful or unmanageable?
♡ Do you have days where you feel overwhelmed by the things you have to do?
♡ Do holidays, friends visiting or days out feel like a burden of planning rather than a joy?

2. What will they think?

I was at the mothers and toddlers group and my son was sat playing happily in one place. All the other children of similar age were off, and he was the only one not crawling. I was really conscious of worrying that he was failing, not achieving now, maybe never in life, far-fetched as that may seem. I went straight home and started working on crawling with him, so he could catch up.

My childminder has always done school drop-off and pick-up. I went to the Christmas nativity and could hear the snide remarks from the other mums... "That's her the one that works full time..."

I was at the playground when my 4 year old threw him-self prostrate on the ground and screamed with all his might about how much he hated me. I gave in and bought him the ice cream, as all the mums were staring.

My 9-year-old daughter had gone off to Guide camp and they called to say she had wet the bed every night. I could hear what they thought of me in their tone of voice.

He just decided to drop out of college to "find himself", no thought of the years of schooling, no thought for me. He's 19, what is there to find?

Mine was the only house that looked a mess. I stopped having people come round, making excuses just so that no one could see how behind I had got with my housework.

♡ Does it matter to you what others think of you and your children?
♡ Can you be outwardly or inwardly affected by what you believe other people will think about you or your children?
♡ Does your concern about others' opinions, about what you think others are thinking about you, ever overshadow how you behave or react to your children?
♡ Have you ever made decisions about what your family will or won't do based not on what you all want, but on what you perceive others or society in general think you should want?
♡ Have you ever cringed at your children's' behaviour, development or achievements, embarrassed by what you believe others will think?

3. Poor me...

I earn more than him, I work longer hours than him and yet my husband is incapable of noticing the mess he creates. He lives in a world where he believes he is helping and yet he is oblivious to the towels, empty mugs, shoes, shopping bags... the list is endless, that he discards randomly across the house. God knows how he would cope with the house and kids if I ever got ill!

I have spent the day dealing with breastfeeding our child, trying to get her to sleep, or to eat and stop crying. Our son has needed constant reassurance and love and yet he [her husband] comes home after I've got them both to bed, upset that I don't jump up to kiss and hug him. He is angry about my lack of affection for him; can't he see I've got nothing left?

34

He tried to look after the kids for the day. They were all high on sugar and greasy chips, queasy from too many hours on a bouncy castle and tearful about broken new, totally unsuitable toys. I get back to them all sat in front of the telly having watched two hours of sport, even our six month old. I just can't trust him to look after them.

They all get up from the table, without a word of thanks. Get on with their day and don't even notice that I planned, created, bought, prepared and served their food, only to have to throw away what was rejected, clear the table and tidy the kitchen, before starting all over again for the next meal.

The list is endless: the washing, drying, ironing, folding, putting away of five people's clothes. Picking up news-papers, football kits, school uniforms and work shirts, dealing with the dust, the dirt, the footprints and grubby hands, the shaving foam and endless stubble in the sink. It wouldn't even occur to him to help.

♡ Have your loved ones ever tried to help you, but the way they do things isn't exactly the same as you would like it, so you just do it anyway, or redo what they have done?

♡ Do you ever end a day feeling resentful and angry at your lack of support and yet you never ask for help?

♡ Have you got to the point where you don't even bother to ask for help any more as no one would remember to do it and you would just have to keep nagging?

♡ Have you allowed people to treat you in a way that you're now dissatisfied with?

4. I feel so bad

It just kept coming back to me, if only I hadn't had the odd glass of wine when I was pregnant, maybe he wouldn't have all these problems. I mean, I never had more than one, but I did maybe once a week have a glass of wine. It's so awful, it is my fault he is suffering.

I handed her over, screaming and clinging to me, she was shouting "Mummy please don't leave me". I was really late so I had to turn and walk away, hearing her screaming for me. I cried all the way to work.

I just turned around for two seconds to pick up his brother when I heard the bump. He fell from the top of the slide and had broken his wrist in two places. I can't tell you how bad I felt.

Finally a day to myself to catch up on shopping for me, I get back into the car to a list of 10 missed calls. I had missed my son's school sports day! Can you believe it? He had no one to watch him and when I arrived he was sat alone with a teacher, waiting for someone to come and get him. What kind of mother am I?

I had to get him out, I couldn't spend one more day living with him, but to hear my child cry every night for their dad made me feel selfish and a terrible mum.

♡ Do you spend long periods of time analysing the effect your actions, choices and decisions have had on your family's wellbeing, long after the decisions and events occurred?

♥ Do you feel guilty about things that have happened to your family and focus on the part you think you played in any problems, placing the greatest blame at your feet?

♥ How much of your time do you spend feeling guilty about something to do with your family?

♥ Do you feel you are always letting someone down: your children, your friends, your work, your partner or yourself?

5. Please let it stop

I had to go downstairs and leave him screaming. I knew if I stayed I would do something I would regret for the rest of my life, but the crying just wouldn't stop and I had no idea what was wrong with him. [Mother of a six-week-old baby at 2 a.m.]

We had been through our holidays with us all having colds and chest infections, each child taking it in turns to wake up coughing, with tonsillitis, followed by conjunctivitis and an ear infection. I had my frequent flyer points at the GP surgery. Now my eldest has started vomiting, closely followed by my husband and now the baby. God it's relentless, I can't cope.

All I have to do is open my mouth and I know my daughter will argue the toss. Whatever I say is "bloody typical" and "ignorant" or just ignored. I can't relax in my own home.

An 8-hour day at the office, home for my children's bath and bed time, international conference call at 8 pm, then start the housework, no break for a cup of tea let alone food...

♡ Do you feel that life is happening to you rather than for you?
♡ How many things in your life feel out of your control?
♡ Does being a mum sometimes feel overwhelming and relentless?

6. That's to be expected, I'm a mum

Breakfast? I don't have breakfast; there is no way I could get them all out of the house and eat myself. I grab something later.

If I get up at 5 I can feel human, have a shower, put my make-up on and be dressed, with the dishwasher empty by the time they all wake up. Of course that means I go to bed at 9, but...

When we have bought all the new school shoes, uni-forms, up-to-date trainers and paid for the school trips, there isn't much left. I went back to work part time so we can hold it all together, I work nights, and get four hours' sleep before the kids wake up. I don't need much; I don't go anywhere really these days.

My weekends? It's breakfast and the dog walk first thing, then take my son to karate and hockey for my daughter at 9, or if it's an away match 10. We have to be back in time for county football in the winter, cricket in the summer, and then to walk the dog before making tea. Sundays are for her dancing competitions and his rugby, my husband has golf. They are all amazingly busy.

I have two children, a dog and my husband works away. My mum is incapacitated and needs me to visit her twice a week and take her food shopping. I'm kept very busy!

♡ Do you feel that it's OK for your needs to come last as you're a mum?

♡ Are your days filled with fulfilling your family's needs rather than your own?

♡ Do you find yourself thinking: if I make personal sacrifices my children can have what they need?

7. Can you believe it?

She was still in her pyjamas at 10 o'clock, the baby was still in a baby-gro, I don't know what had gone wrong that morning but she was really behind. [Oops, she must have been looking through my window on any non-school day]

There she was, six months pregnant, stood outside smoking, while her daughter was running wild inside. It was appalling.

She has gone back to work and put her son in full-time childcare. She doesn't even give him his breakfast. I mean, why have children?

She lets her daughter stay out all hours and lets her boyfriend sleep in her room at weekends. I would never let my daughter do that.

She just lets him run riot, he hits other children and pushes them and she does nothing. [A mum discussing the mother of a 2 year old]

♡ How often do you give your opinion and those of your friends when examining the lives of other mums?

♡ Do you believe your way of parenting and that of your peers is the right way, and any way that differs is less correct?

♡ Do you often have an opinion on other people's choices, which you voice to others?

♡   ♡   ♡

OK, truth time: did you recognise yourself in any or many of those scenarios?

How are you feeling about your scores in each of these areas?

Take time to reflect and listen: what is your inner voice busy saying right now?

These are not extreme scenarios, they are real-life comments from mums I talked to and who agreed to contribute to the book. I'm not saying any of these comments are right or wrong, I am simply encouraging you to observe them and how they relate to you.

Each of these examples relates to a potential inter-fear-ance that can affect the level of your performance, in this case your satisfaction and happiness as a mum. Each is a mindset hurdle, a barrier to clear thinking and to reaching your potential as a mum, or accepting the mum you are.

ARE YOU READY TO BEGIN?

How many days do you find yourself exhausted, from either embracing and enjoying your day or enduring and coping through it? Do you finally drop into the sofa with a much-needed glass of wine, a coffee or some snacks and disappear into someone else's life – a soap character, a documentary maker or a reality TV personality?

Just as children watch the TV and films and become the characters they have seen, we do the same as adults on a very small level, climbing temporarily into the characters' lives and switching off our own. It can feel like a blissful relief.

Or maybe you jump onto the computer. You could be catching up on or continuing your day's work, or disappearing into a cyberworld where you can anonymously be witty, intelligent, a great friend and an entirely better you. You could catch up on gossip, chat with friends, sell off unwanted items (or buy more unwanted items!), plan holidays, or dream of redecorating or other projects.

You lose yourself until you finally realise the time, haul yourself from the sofa and crawl off to bed. Maybe you sleep well, sheer exhaustion bringing you peace, or you enjoy the rest that comes from being satisfied and replete. Alternatively you may struggle to sleep or stay asleep, worrying about your children, relationships, finances or the concerns of the day ahead. You then wake to another day and start all over again.

How often do you catch glimpses of what is happening inside you?

How often are you snappy and irritable, sad or frustrated, with no clear reason?

Do you ever find your mind or thoughts drifting to a place in the future where you are fitter, more organised, attending a class regularly, sexier, healthier, a different person?

Do you then console yourself with the fact you're so busy right now you couldn't possibly make any changes, but that you will fulfil that image of the future one day? Satisfied with this explanation and justification, you carry on into another fun- or stress-filled day.

My challenge to you is to take action as you become more self-aware. If you realise you have feelings of frustration, disappointment, sadness, guilt or even despair about your-self, they won't get quieter or fade away as your children grow and your life gets busier, or your children move on and your life gets quieter.

The discontent will get louder!

Feelings are messengers from your inner voice, your self-awareness, to you about how you are coping on the inside. They are signals for help or attention that will sneak through even the most positive day. They are the communication from your inner thoughts, to guide and alert you to what is and what isn't working in your life right now, trying to talk to you, asking you to listen.

Or maybe your life as a mum isn't this bleak: you may be very contented with the majority of your life, fulfilled, motivated and satisfied with yourself. For you, my question would be: is your behaviour to others always resourceful?

Are you sharing the beneficial aspects of yourself and benefiting those around you more than you are taking from others?

All emotions, whether negative or positive, have a pur-pose. In every case, ask yourself: "Are my thoughts, feelings, actions and behaviours resourceful, useful and taking me and my life in the direction I want to go?"

HEAR YOUR INNER VOICE

Life these days is very loud. We fill our bodies and our minds with radios, CDs, iPods, MP3s, television, the inter-net, cars, coffee houses, pubs, winebars, playgrounds, indoor play areas – all of these create a continuous hum of back-ground noise. Combine this with the noise children bring with their cries, their laughter, their questions and their fears, and peace can be a distant memory.

And yet one noise that will continue to try to be heard through it all is your inner feelings. Your inner voice, unheard and unlistened to, will start to fight back and all those unheard and unacknowledged emotions will begin to leak out.

The best way to demonstrate what is happening and why is to use the image of an iceberg.

In our day-to-day lives what is externally seen and shared with others is our behaviour and our results. "Results" has a different meaning for every mum, but for now I would like to gauge results as not only the task-based achievements – the three loads of washing, the three fairly healthy meals, maybe a good day's work, the trip to the park giving all of you a dose of fresh air and the time spent reading and doing homework with your children – although they are important if they rate as achievements to you. That's what is above the surface of the water, the tip of the iceberg. What I mean by results here is your awareness of how you feel you are performing against the idealised picture you have of a good mum. This is the rest of the iceberg,

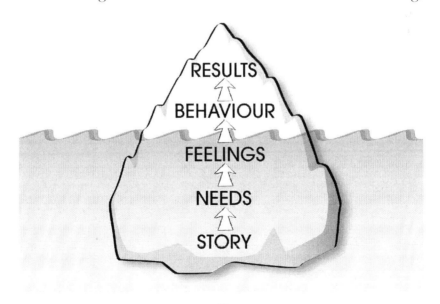

underneath the water. We will go on to examine all three of the elements under the water line, including the concept of stories – hold on, we will get there!

Start listening and assessing whether your inner self is happy with you. What is happening beneath the surface of your iceberg – what is your body trying to tell you?

What are you thinking?

How you are feeling?

To do this I do need you to turn off other noises for a while. It is easy to ignore your inner thoughts and feelings when you can hide in a world of "too busy" or "I'll do it tomorrow" excuses.

I know all these reasons, justification and excuses feel very valid at the time, and I promise I've either used them myself or heard them from others. Some of you may have very good reasons why now is not the time for you to change. However, my warning to you would be this:

How soon not now, becomes never. —**Martin Luther**

Our inner psychology is designed to accept the excuses/reasons we give for not doing things and it will accept them for a lifetime. (I cover this in detail at the end of the book.)

Every time you accept an excuse you add a tick to your inner "I'll never achieve what I want" box and that frustration accumulates, eventually leaking out in unexpected grumpiness, irritability and anger with yourself and others.

Thoughts and feelings *never* go away. You can only bury them, where they will thrive, grow and fight back stronger and louder.

Feelings buried alive never die. —**Karol K Truman**

"I don't sit down until 9 at night, the last thing I want to do is start thinking!"

"I'm just too tired to think about anything, I'm just going to watch an hour of telly."

"Let me just go on Facebook, get my emails and check I am up to date with everyone."

"I won't sleep if I don't have my switch-off time and a glass of wine to turn off my day and my mind."

"I would like to be happier with myself but I'm doing OK, my life's not that bad."

"I'll just get through my child's teething, starting school, his football season, this term, the holidays, her exams, his wedding."

Let me share something with you; One of my friends said about her mum after she had died:

My mum was always a little sad, she always seemed sort of discontented and frustrated through her life, she just seemed unfulfilled and I never got the chance to ask her why.

My friend was sad that that is how she remembers her mum.

45

EXERCISE 3
HOW WILL YOUR CHILDREN REMEMBER YOU?

Psychology has shown that this exercise is one sure-fire way to analyse whether any part of you does want to change.

Imagine it is the day of your funeral. You are there, floating above all the people who have shared your life.
　　Your life has ended with you being exactly who you are today. Tomorrow never did come and you never did any of those things you said you would.

♡ How do you feel?
♡ Has your life made you proud and contented?
♡ Do you have any regrets about any of the things you have not done?

Your children are grown up and adults themselves, and your family, friends and work colleagues are all gathered to say goodbye to you.

♡ What are they saying about you? (A quick check-in with yourself here: if people were talking about what they actually observed in your consistent behaviours over your lifetime rather than what they feel they had to say, what would they say?)
♡ What qualities of yours are your children reflecting on?
♡ What are they listing as your achievements, your successes?
♡ Are you proud and contented with what they are saying?
♡ Are you proud of the impact and contribution you made to their lives?

♡ Did you find this exercise in any way painful or challenging?
♡ Are you genuinely satisfied that you are living a life you would look back on with joy and pride?
♡ Are you living the amazing, satisfying achieving life that you planned for yourself?
♡ Have you ever had a plan or given yourself time to plan your life?

If your answer to any of the last three questions in the exercise is no, then there is no justification, reason or excuse not to change that is good enough, if not for you then for your children. (Yes, for all those grumpy inner voices out there, I am resorting to emotional blackmail.)

Believe me, I'm not coming from any place of perfection, I am not telling you what to do, because I fight every day to stay on track with my goals and some days I find myself distinctly off track. The only person who knows if you want to do this is you.

What I will say is, whatever your beliefs: **this is *now* and this is the only life you have. Without being morbid or scaring you, there may not be a tomorrow.**

You have to decide if you're going to spend one more night escaping into the television, computer, biscuit barrel or glass of wine. Or are you ready now to look at the person, the mum, the woman you are?

When you reach the end of your life, do you want to be one of the people who are glad they did, or one of the people who wish they had?

There are many ways to measure success; not least of which is the way your child describes you when talking to a friend.

ABOVE THE WATER LINE

When gaining awareness of your achievements, your successes and what others think of you, you are examining the layers of the iceberg above the water line – what can be seen externally and interpreted by others. The world of personal development and coaching has been full for years with work on developing how you think, act and strive to achieve these results. The power of positive thought has been drummed into us for the last two decades, encouraging us to "think positive" and not to take no for an answer, not to accept failure and to win. These theories all have their place and for many have brought amazing results.

My experience as a mum has shown me that positive thinking does not cut it where two boys under 3 are concerned. If I did in fact convince myself that everything was going to be perfect and positive, I was brought back down to earth with a bigger bump when it was not. I was sitting in hospital holding my seriously ill baby when my fear and despair caused me to revisit the tools I had taught executives, to re-examine the fundamental elements of A TRUTH and compare them with what I was living in reality. I realised that hearing and seeing only the facts of a situation, without bias, exaggeration or judgement, gives a more realistic solution to facing the challenges of motherhood and moving forward. To do this we must now start to look at what is happening inside us, under the water level of the iceberg – we need to turn to the next step of A TRUTH, our thoughts and feelings.

But first, an interlude to look at problems that face many mums: depression and tiredness.

DEPRESSION AND TIREDNESS

When acknowledging your feelings about your real life as a mum, it's important to assess whether something more serious is going on than a general difficulty in coping.

THIS FEELS TOO SCARY

I'm sure you don't need me to tell you that as mums, especially just after giving birth, we have these amazing influences on our emotions and moods known as hormones. They can enhance and expand feelings of joy and exaggerate and explode any lows or worries. These alone can be hard enough to navigate, but what is crucial to clarify is whether any of the feelings you have about yourself as a mum are actually more significant.

Depression is the result of a chemical imbalance within the brain, when some of the brain's neurotransmitters or chemicals become depleted and cause sadness, anxiety and a range of other symptoms. The medical belief is that this is as clear-cut a diagnosis as that low levels of iron equate to anaemia. Using the definition supplied by ICD 10 (International Classification of Diseases 10th revision), it is a sustained low or sad mood with a loss of interest or pleasure. Often because of the very impact of the chemical imbalance, we have no insight into how low our state of mind has got. We will all over our lifetime feel like that sometimes, but it is the depth and the length of time you have been feeling low that matter.

Mental illness and depression are subjects that invoke strong feelings and views. Having worked in the field of

49

depression for over 10 years, I know that realising and acknowledging that there is a medical condition causing your feelings often gives people a starting point and some clarity from which to work. That is surely far better than living with the fear that something may or may not be wrong. Depression is a treatable condition and often diagnosis is a route to new ways of thinking and feeling.

There are many assessment tools that healthcare professional use to assess and diagnose depression and they are very simple and clear. Should you believe, suspect or have fears that you may be depressed, the ideas and suggestions in this book are still relevant and useful, but I would strongly recommend that you seek medical or professional help. If as you work through the book one of the exercises or chapters creates feelings or thoughts that you feel are too strong to handle alone, seek out a professional to work them through with you.

If you are living with a diagnosis of depression and working through it with medical or psychological help, the book will be a good source for building your own emotional skill set alongside any counselling or pharmaceuticals you may be using. Believe me, many, many great mums have lived through and overcome depression and you can too, so ask for help if you need it.

BUT GILL, I'M SO TIRED

The most recorded reason for seeing a GP is TATT, being tired all the time. It's a challenge close to the hearts of most parents, particularly new mums as they feed and support their baby 24 hours a day. The evidence about lack of sleep is indisputable: it's responsible for low immunity, low mood, irritability and many more physical challenges. Many mums find that the pressures of motherhood, even once the children are sleeping, bring periods of insomnia and worry through the night, again leading to exhaustion and weariness.

My second son Jake did not sleep longer than three hours at any one time for the first nine months of his life. He didn't cope too badly, as he could snooze at the drop of a hat through the day and catch up on his sleep as I pushed the buggy, shopped or drove. But with a 2 year old to keep happy as well, I lived in a constant fog for all that time. My immune system became weakened and I caught every bug my eldest son managed to collect at nursery and a few all of my own. I forgot anything I didn't write down, and often those things I had. But most importantly, remaining aware of my emotional state and keeping control of my needs and emotions was doubly hard through a cloud of tiredness.

Be kind to yourself if lack of sleep is an issue for you. It is a real problem, it deserves respect and acknowledgement, and battling through it may not be enough. Again, if you suspect you need it, get help. Read this book and use the techniques as well as you can, but don't berate yourself if you struggle to remain aware at all times. If you right now or at any time when reading this book think you need a good sleep more, *just go and sleep!*

MINDSET IN A MINUTE
BECOMING AWARE

Learn to listen to yourself, your intuition, your inner voice. It could be shouting very loud for help. Turn off your busy, hectic, noisy life for a second and make time to hear it.

Negative events in life will always happen to you, you have no control over them. What you can control is how you respond to each event and the mood you carry forward afterwards.

Build your awareness of what a "good mum" looks like to you, from your childhood, your peer groups, your own mum. Set a desired state for yourself.

Become aware of the stereotypes and labels that society, the media, your employer, your friends and you place on mothers: your opinions or judgements on full-time mums, mums who choose to work, mums who work because they have to, single mums. Awareness of your judgements brings clarity of your measures of what a "good mum" looks like and how you feel you are measuring up against this invisible standard.

Begin to realise that you start out with full, 100% potential to be the woman and the mum you want to be. Inter-fear-ances happen to you, or you choose them and they have an impact on your achievements and results.

Potential – inter-fear-ances = performance

Start to become aware of your inter-fear-ances, your limitations and the impact they have had.

Now is the time to decide if you are happy. Do you end each day satisfied and at peace? If not, are you ready to change?

Imagine it is the day of your funeral. You are there, floating above all the people who have shared your life.

Your life has ended with you being exactly who you are today. Tomorrow never did come and you never did any of those things you said you would.

How do you feel?

CHAPTER 2

THOUGHTS AND FEELINGS

You probably believe that your thoughts are your own, and that they are real. They come from within you and they arrive instantaneously without any conscious altering. However, one fundamental step we will take together is realising that not only can our thoughts be leftover baggage from painful, stressful or challenging events or situations in our lives, they can also be dysfunctional – and completely false.

We need to start recognising and changing the inherent negative thinking patterns and outdated beliefs about ourselves that we are carrying, formed from other people's views. Then we can start to look at life from a new perspective, with our own, new thoughts – and then we can change our lives, should we wish.

OH, SHE IS SO EMOTIONAL!

Women are stereotypically labelled as the more emotional sex. The view that we are unpredictable, prone to influence from our hormones, moods, sulking and random snapping is the meat of many a joke and tale of woe. However, I have watched the business world slowly change and start to accept that having a greater level of emotional intelligence is not only a strength but essential in both leading and getting the most from others. Exactly the same is true of mums, both working and full time

I believe that both men and women live across a spectrum of the ability to analyse thoughts, feelings and emotions and the depth of experience with which they do so. What women do often struggle to do is to take time actually to listen to what we are thinking and feeling.

Psychology has established that thoughts, feelings and emotions are the body's signals or messengers about what we need. They are a sign from within that something is happening that has caused us to feel a particular way, which may be either positive or negative. Starting to listen to those thoughts and feelings and responding to the needs attached to them is the key to reducing inter-fear-ance in our lives.

WHAT I FEEL, NOT WHAT I THINK

We need to make one important distinction. Feelings are the messengers of our thoughts, the signal that something is affecting us emotionally. They are personal; they come as reactions to what is happening to us. However, how often do you hear yourself or others say:

> I feel that he should know better
> I feel like a failure
> I feel inadequate as a mum

These aren't feelings, they're actually judgements – statements of our thoughts, not the expression of what we are actually feeling. For a feeling to be acknowledged and released it needs to be identified and labelled with the emotion it carries, not attributed to the thought it comes from. Let me explain.

Marshall Rosenberg is a true role model for me who is working to change the way we communicate with each other to build a more compassionate world. I have training in his non-violent communication approach and will continue to use it for the rest of my life.

He proposes that with statements such as those above we are placing a thought onto our feelings. We are making a judgement, an assessment or conclusion about the feeling and therefore we are not truly listening to what we feel.

Likewise, we often place responsibility for our feelings on others, by saying something like: "I feel you don't love me." Rosenberg explains that this is you expressing what you think the other person is thinking or doing/not doing, not what you are feeling.

It is very easy to confuse our feelings with what the other person is doing or not doing to us; in fact, often it's become a habit. When we say "I feel used, ignored, taken advantage of, rejected", we are describing our perceptions of the other person's actions or inactions.

Mary's husband gets an invite on a Friday afternoon to join a game of golf the next morning, not only at the new prestigious golf club, but with the senior partners in his organisation. Making the assessment that it was "too good a career opportunity to miss", he agrees to go, without checking with Mary first. The weekends, especially Saturday mornings, are normally a respite for Mary, since Alex gets up with the kids and gives her a lie-in and a break. Saturday dawns and he sets off at 7 the next morning. Her internal dialogue starts: "I feel totally abandoned, he is so selfish and thoughtless" (in fact her language was far stronger, but you get the idea!).

What Mary is actually describing is what she believes Alex has done to her: left her alone with the kids on her usual morning off. She is saying what he *is*, putting a judgemental label on his actions. Both may be true, but what she is probably really feeling is angry, both that he made the decision without consulting her and at her disappointment that her once-a-week lie-in is being taken away. She may be feeling exhausted by just the thought of another day alone with the kids and sad that Alex didn't realise how much she needed a break.

Mary can either believe that her feelings are due to what her husband has done to her by playing golf that Saturday morning (and therefore feel that her happiness is totally out of her control), or she can acknowledge her true feelings of anger, exhaustion and sadness and decide what, if anything, she can do using her personal control to get back into a resourceful state.

The reason I am asking you to truly hear what you are feeling is that to become more at peace, to stop your internal discontentment, you have to allow your feelings to be heard and then to dissipate. To do that, you have to hear, acknowledge and know what they are.

Imagine you have snapped at your children ten times and are starting to berate yourself for being a "moody cow". You then ask yourself what you're feeling, what is wrong, and discover that you're actually feeling sad about a conversation you had with your friend earlier, a sadness which once acknowledged allows your calmness to return. Take it from me, it is an unbelievable relief. You finally understand why you're feeling what you're feeling.

The bottom line in a perfect world is this:

Nobody or nothing makes us feel anything. **Every feeling, every emotion, comes directly from ourselves, either consciously or unconsciously.**

Before you explode, just think about it... The reality for us mere mortals is that others' actions do affect us: they create thoughts which in turn create feelings. The learning comes when we develop our self-awareness to a level that means we can quickly move from an unconscious reaction to others' actions to a more considered response, releasing our feelings to allow our distress from those actions to reduce.

To start to build an awareness of specific feelings, I am including the Center for Non-Violent Communication's dictionary of feelings. This will help you to articulate, acknowledge and then answer your feelings and start to identify your emotional state.

> *One's suffering disappears when one lets oneself go, when one yields – even to sadness. —**Antoine de Saint-Exupéry, Southern Mail, 1929, translated from French by Curtis Cate***

EXERCISE 4
UNDERSTANDING HOW YOU FEEL

Think back to the last time you felt strongly about something. Maybe you saw it on the news: the death of a child through parental abuse, a parent's loss through war or illness, or casualties from a natural disaster. Or maybe it was frustration at a fellow driver, a queue in the supermarket, your boss's feedback or a random comment from another mum at the school pick-up.

Look at the list of feelings overleaf and write down all the ones that apply to how you felt.

LOVE YOU MUM

AFFECTIONATE
compassionate
friendly
loving
open-hearted
sympathetic
tender
warm

CONFIDENT
empowered
open
proud
safe
secure

ENGAGED
absorbed
alert
curious
engrossed
enchanted
entranced
fascinated
interested
intrigued
involved
spellbound
stimulated

INSPIRED
amazed
awed
wonder

EXCITED
amazed
animated
ardent
aroused
astonished
dazzled
eager
energetic
enthusiastic
giddy
invigorated
lively

passionate
surprised
vibrant

EXHILARATED
blissful
ecstatic
elated
enthralled
exuberant
radiant
rapturous
thrilled

GRATEFUL
appreciative
moved
thankful
touched

HOPEFUL
expectant
encouraged
optimistic

JOYFUL
amused
delighted
glad
happy
jubilant
pleased
tickled

PEACEFUL
calm
clear-headed
comfortable
centred
content
equanimous
fulfilled
mellow
quiet
relaxed
relieved
satisfied
serene

still
tranquil
trusting

REFRESHED
enlivened
rejuvenated
renewed
rested
restored
revived

AFRAID
apprehensive
dread
foreboding
frightened
mistrustful
panicked
petrified
scared
suspicious
terrified
wary
worried

ANNOYED
aggravated
dismayed
disgruntled
displeased
exasperated
frustrated
impatient
irritated
irked

ANGRY
enraged
furious
incensed
indignant
irate
livid
outraged
resentful

cont.

AVERSION
animosity
appalled
contempt
disgusted
dislike
hate
horrified
hostile
repulsed

CONFUSED
ambivalent
baffled
bewildered
dazed
hesitant
lost
mystified
perplexed
puzzled
torn

DISCONNECTED
alienated
aloof
apathetic
bored
cold
detached
distant
distracted
indifferent
numb
removed
uninterested
withdrawn

DISQUIET
agitated
alarmed
discombobulated
disconcerted
disturbed
perturbed
rattled
restless
shocked

startled
surprised
troubled
turbulent
turmoil
uncomfortable
uneasy
unnerved
unsettled
upset

EMBARRASSED
ashamed
chagrined
flustered
guilty
mortified
self-conscious

FATIGUE
beat
burnt out
depleted
exhausted
lethargic
listless
sleepy
tired
weary
worn out

PAIN
agony
anguished
bereaved
devastated
grief
heartbroken
hurt
lonely
miserable
regretful
remorseful

SAD
depressed
dejected
despair

despondent
disappointed
discouraged
disheartened
forlorn
gloomy
heavy hearted
hopeless
melancholy
unhappy
wretched

TENSE
anxious
cranky
distressed
distraught
edgy
fidgety
frazzled
irritable
jittery
nervous
overwhelmed
restless
stressed out

VULNERABLE
fragile
guarded
helpless
insecure
leery
reserved
sensitive
shaky

YEARNING
envious
jealous
longing
nostalgic
pining
wistful

In many circumstances, how we respond to an event or a situation creates a multifaceted spectrum of thoughts and feelings. Often these intermingle and melt into a pot of intensely complicated emotions that create the way we react and respond.

By starting to separate out, examine and identify our true thoughts and feelings, rather than the assumed or implied ones, we can start to really see what is going on inside.

We start by owning what we are thinking and how that causes us to behave.

I have often said: "It's my hormones making me act like this." Or similarly: "They [my boss, my mum, my husband] made me angry/sad." Doing so accepts and excuses any aggressive, moody or snappy behaviour as not my fault.

Mums I talk to have come up with a variety of seemingly valid reasons as to why they are moody, tetchy, snappy and cross. But unless we have a chemical imbalance within our mental state which leaves us unable to rationalise, reset and rebalance what we are thinking, feeling and saying, we have to own up that, having been triggered by someone behaving negatively or a particular event, **we *choose* to snap, shout, sulk or scream at those around us.**

Often it is far from a conscious decision. In fact, more often than not we subsequently feel frustrated about and regret our behaviour. This is a clear illustration of an unconscious thought creating an inner feeling which leaks out to behaviour above the water line.

Underneath this outer communication there will be thoughts and feelings we have not acknowledged or listened to. They may well be created from a situation or person external to ourselves, but what we have chosen to do is to mindlessly ignore our feelings and what they are attempting to show us, and created a bad mood, which infects the rest of our day and many of those we come into contact with.

Taking responsibility for your happiness also means taking responsibility for your sadness, your loneliness, your frustration, your pain. The first step to achieving this is starting to listen to and identify what you are thinking.

EXERCISE 5
WHY DID I DO THAT?

Think about the last time you lost your temper, or snapped at a loved one or colleague and regretted it.

♡ What else had happened in your day?

♡ Was the person you lost your temper with the original cause of your bad mood?

♡ Was it something they had done that day, or were you angry about a previous event or series of events?

♡ Was the level of loss of temper valid to the outburst?

♡ What were you feeling inside and why?

Clare had been snapping at her children for a number of days. She was finding her 3-year-old daughter's attention seeking and tantrums draining and wearing. She was attempting to demonstrate to her daughter that a calm, thoughtful approach to her tantrums was helpful and yet she was losing her cool as much as her daughter was.

When Clare and I sat down and examined what else was happening for her, it emerged that her husband had taken up a new keep-fit regime. He was coming home late after the gym, buzzing with energy and positivity and looking slimmer and more confident. Clare was not only feeling jealous and resentful at her husband's ability to have the time to exercise, she was also feeling insecure and sad at her own inability to feel that good about herself. It was multifaceted: she was proud of her husband but unable to share that with him out of the deep-seated fear that he was improving and she was staying still.

She loved her children and her job, but resented the fact that she had no time to herself to exercise and start to rebuild her self-esteem. Her negative thoughts and feelings were building within her and showing themselves in her response to her daughter as well as influencing her behaviour towards her husband.

Once Clare had listened to and acknowledged those thoughts and feelings, she talked to her husband both about her fears and about her need for time to start exercising too. She then found that her daughter's tantrums invoked a feeling of pride about her strong self-expression. She made a real move forward in her relationship with both her daughter and her husband.

A basic law of physics is that energy once created never dies, unless it's re-created as the next form of energy. What this teaches us and I see every day in my clients is the following.

If an event or someone else's comment, conversation or action has caused you to have negative thoughts, this causes negative feelings to be created. If those feelings are not labelled or acknowledged, they will not simply fade away and die. They will either sit in an internal box somewhere, stored away, being topped up every time the same person or event affects you, simmering quietly, sometimes for years – only to burst out, often completely inappropriately and out of proportion, in a discussion or argument with that person or about that event. Or they join forces, gather strength and explode daily in the form of moodiness and snappiness, or implode and create statements, actions or behaviours too frightful ever to explain away. This is not being too emotional or moody, it is purely the result of not learning the skill of labelling, acknowledging and acting on the feelings you have when they happen.

More importantly, long-term unacknowledged feelings also hurt you, creating within you constant *dis*-ease.

As a mum, you are not necessarily more hormonally challenged, more irrational, more moody, you are just beset by so much noise around you that you are unable to stop and listen to what you are actually thinking and feeling and acknowledge it. Believe me, I've heard the whole gamut of emotions, from pure resentment and sometimes hatred of the life that being a mum has brought, the worn-down acknowledgement of perceived drudgery, monotony, boredom at sharing day after day with little people who at first can't communicate in any other way than with their bowels and tears, improving to ignorance and even disdain as they grow, and to the disbelief at the stratospheric levels of pure, unlimited, unbridled, unconditional love for little people who bring nothing but joy and learning as they grow. And that's just in one day! We all travel along a spectrum between these extremes with every new moment we encounter as mums.

What we feel has a direct effect on how we behave. What do those around us see from above the water line? Taking responsibility for the behaviours that our children, family, colleagues and friends see requires us to start listening and acting on what we are feeling.

EXERCISE 6
STARTING TO LISTEN AND RESPOND TO YOUR NEEDS

Keep the book open, and wait...

This is an exercise for the next time you start to act in a way that you have enough awareness to realise is dispropor-tionate to the situation or circumstances you are in. For exam-ple, you are acting aggressively towards your partner, children or colleague. You are eating something that doesn't fit with your goals for fitness. You are sitting down in front of the TV or computer when you know you have other things you want to be doing.

Stop and ask yourself:

♡ What am I thinking?

♡ Is anything wrong?
♡ What has happened, and how has it made me feel?
(I sometimes use the NVC list to help me correctly label what is happening for me.)

♡ What are those feelings and what are they telling me?

Listen to the feelings you have identified, understand them and empathise with yourself for feeling them. Work out if there is anything you can do to alleviate or answer those thoughts and feelings that could help your mood.

This is the first step. You are breaking a pattern of behaviour that has been automatic for you, probably for most of your life. You are becoming self-aware and making choices from how you are thinking and feeling.

You are changing, you are growing and developing, you are finding *you*!

BUT MUMMY, I NEED IT!

What our children need often seems very clear and obvious to them. They need to have another sweet and when they're told that they can't have one as their mum thinks they've had enough sugar, they fully experience the depth of their feelings about not getting what they require, be that a heart-felt round of pitiful tears or the full-blown sulk or tantrum of the hard-done-by toddler or teenager.

To our children, needs are simple requirements that they feel strong emotions about when they are not met. An infant's need to eat, sleep, be dry and warm is natural, in-built and instinctive from the minute they are born and they quickly learn within their communication capabilities how to make their needs known.

Somewhere on the journey from childhood to adulthood, we all learn about the apparent inappropriateness of strong emotional responses to our needs not being met. We temper and restrict both our reactions to unmet needs and our feelings, and in time we lose the ability to hear what we need.

Society has built a structure of blame and seems to teach us to attribute to other people the fault for our needs not being met, rather than teaching us to directly acknowledge and take responsibility for what we need.

I hear people express their needs indirectly all the time. "Nobody cares about how I feel!", "He never listens to me", "She doesn't understand me", "They just take advantage of me" – in each of these statements the person is attributing their unmet need to be heard, understood or respected to someone else's actions.

Like the infant we were at birth, all of us have inherent needs, which cause pain if they are not met. Our needs grow and become more complicated than the basic needs for food, love and warmth, and yet the impact of not having our basic needs met is still as painful as the cry of a hungry child.

We need autonomy, integrity, love, respect, acceptance and much more. Should our inherent needs for these things not be met, our negative thoughts and feelings only grow.

Nevertheless, throughout history the image of a loving woman has been associated with sacrifice and the denial of her own needs to take care of others. It seems to be an unwritten rule that when you become a mum it is your duty to put others, particularly your children, first, placing your own needs as at least secondary, but in many instances as unimportant.

This view is reflected in the sacrifice of buying a child-friendly home rather than a glamorous penthouse, or turning down a stimulating promotion to stay available to your children, but also in the daily little things: letting your child have the last yoghurt of your favourite flavour, or using the remainder of the pint of milk for their cereal in the morning and you not having a coffee.

When I speak to men and discuss their needs, I often hear a very different view. They are much better at stating their needs and on insisting on getting them met. Rosenberg's work echoes this. In contrast, women internalise their needs, negate their needs repeatedly and don't actually state clearly what their needs are. Here's an example.

Tina felt that she was continually snapping at her husband. She would explode at him, rant about his lack of effort around the house, his lack of understanding. She felt remorseful and apologised to him, blaming her hormones following the birth of their third child and claiming the pressure of looking after three children and holding down her job was getting to her. When he hugged her, said he forgave her and made her a cup of tea, she just felt more resentment build.

All of this was exaggerated by her thought that she had shared her challenges and he still didn't give her support. She felt that in her tearful apologies and justifications of the struggle she was having with the stresses of being a mum to three, working and managing a house, she was clearly showing her husband what she needed.

However, her husband heard an apology for her behaviour towards him, not her anger at what he was not doing. What he was not hearing was what she actually needed, because she was not clearly stating it.

Taking responsibility for our feelings is about being specific about what we need, not expecting others to be mind readers. I look at making clear requests to meet our needs later, but the essence is that those around us will only hear our needs if we share clearly what they are.

Tina had a need for support, both physically around the house and emotionally, and she wanted her husband to hear that she was feeling sad about how she sometimes snapped at him. When she finally clarified for him what her needs were, and she made the requests required to meet those needs, he was able to start supporting her in the way she required.

Often we as mums take on the role of caretaker for the family, acting as a martyr, controlling and organising everything for everyone and not stopping to organise things for ourselves and meet our own needs.

On one level we will have made an unconscious decision to put our children's and family's needs first, but we will also be having an inner battle. Our own needs do not go away or lessen any more than feelings do.

Someone who is continually not meeting their own needs will eventually begin to feel the effects of ignoring them. We will start to have internal discussions about fairness, or what we deserve for putting ourselves last all the time, what others should be giving or doing for us in return for all that we do. Finally, these unmet needs and the judgements that they have created begin to leak out – normally not with the people we are negating our needs for, the children, but with our partners, colleagues or other people in our support network.

We unconsciously expect others to see how hard we are working and wait for them to treat us accordingly. We become, angry, resentful, snappy and moody at what others have not done for us, but we never actually ask for or clarify what we would like or expect.

I continually hear fellow mums moan about all the things their partners haven't done for them, but when asked if they have ever explained specifically what they would like and why, they retort that surely "They should know, I have told them often enough!" As we all tell our children, being asked, clearly with a please, and assuming, demanding or being told are two very different things.

THE DRAMA TRIANGLE

Let me clarify what is happening. The diagram opposite represents a very simplified and adapted part of Transactional Analysis, originally created by the respected psychiatrist and teacher Stephen Karpman. He calls it the "drama triangle". My years of coaching have reinforced his speculation that to some extent all of us sit on one of the corners of a triangle in certain contexts of our lives.

In the bottom left-hand corner of the triangle sit caretakers, rescuers – mums?

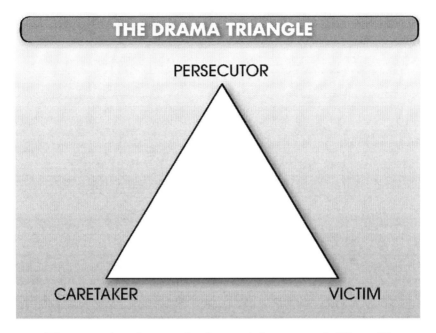

They tend to have a high need for control. They like to get things done and get them done properly, for example making sure that key stuff is achieved for the smooth running of the home and at work. Some have very high standards or perfection patterns and if things are not done to their standard or the way they think will work best, they worry. Their drive for perfection often comes from wanting the best, both for themselves and for those around them, and their drive to care is very strong. They may unwittingly gain self-confidence and self-esteem from rescuing and supporting others and frequently can be heard to say with affection: "Oh, they are hopeless, I have to do everything for them."

The caretaker has created a pattern of taking responsibility for others and putting others before themselves. In relationships and at work they take responsibility for everything getting done and happening correctly. This can be fine for a short while: they caretake and mother everyone,

71

including adults (sometimes their own parents). But inevitably after a period of time their frustration builds as more work leads to more responsibility, and eventually they have to ask others to take on important tasks for them.

Alison was going out for a day at a spa for her friends' hen weekend and leaving her kids with their dad. She had spent all week preparing: instant healthy food for the kids, plenty of clean ironed clothes, a list of activities around town that they could do. She had set up a bag of appropriate toys, buckets and spades, swimsuits etc. for whichever option they chose. She reminded her husband at least five times that he had to sterilise the baby's bottles and not let the eldest go in the sun without his hat. She got out of the shower the morning of the hen do, to see her eldest in his Batman suit for the day and her husband dressing their youngest in his pyjama top to go out. She went ballistic: "One thing, that's all you had to do, get them dressed this morning, and you can't even get that right!"

A caretaker who starts to feel "I do everything for them, they never help, they are useless" begins to slide across the bottom of the triangle towards being a victim. They commence an inner dialogue of: "Poor me, I am the only one who ever gets anything done, I work so hard and I get no support. No one even offers to help any more and when I ask them they get it wrong. What about me, my needs, my free time? It's so unfair!"

The caretaker has taken such levels of control from those around them that they have disempowered them, creating a state of learned helplessness. This state is caused by others trying to do things, attempting to help but being derided for getting it wrong, not being good enough or just not doing it the way the caretaker wants, leading to a sense of failure and resentment and fear of trying to help, which

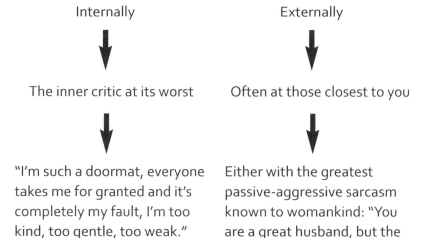

Internally   Externally

The inner critic at its worst   Often at those closest to you

"I'm such a doormat, everyone takes me for granted and it's completely my fault, I'm too kind, too gentle, too weak."

Either with the greatest passive-aggressive sarcasm known to womankind: "You are a great husband, but the dishwasher won't empty itself, you know."
Or cold, blind, aggressive fury, either inwardly or externally: "You are a selfish, stupid, hopeless..."

perpetuates and decreases further the lack of support for the caretaker and creates a vicious circle – or triangle in this instance. Does this ring any bells?

Sat in the victim corner, the caretaker starts to fester and fume. How long they stay there depends on their emotions, the context, history and their mindset, but fairly quickly they climb up to the top of the triangle: the persecutor. This can erupt in two ways, as illustrated above.

These reactions are often far greater in their ferocity than the "crime" that sparked them off deserved, and they can viciously wound those around, or our own self-esteem. All this from the sheer force of the thoughts and feelings created by our unmet needs over time.

Sadly, for inherent caretakers, the anger subsides or gets overshadowed by a need to control again and get things back on track. Now, filled with remorse and guilt, the care-taker slips back to their usual role, taking up the slack and starting the whole cycle all over again.

EXERCISE 7
ARE YOU ON THE TRIANGLE?

♡ Do you ever undo or redo a household or work task that someone helping has done for you?

♡ Is it often easier to do something yourself, rather than try to explain what you need from someone else?

♡ Do you prefer to handle the majority of admin tasks within your household as you know they get done properly? (Or does your partner hold a caretaking pattern in this area?)

♡ Do you predominantly plan, book and organise family events, holidays, weekends away, social activities?

♡ Do you occasionally simply feel resentful or angry at the lack of support from those around you?

♡ Do you despair at the level of incompetence of those around you, carrying out tasks that you have to do every day?

If you answer "yes" to some of these questions, the chances are that, maybe only in a small way, you have slipped into the role of a family caretaker. Believe me, it is easily done as a mum.

The first step towards both relieving yourself of the strain of this role and building up the confidence and abilities of those around you (yes, you may have been that controlling) is to accept that you are doing this.

I have no 12-step programme, no Caretakers Anonymous meeting. What I do have is a promise that by following the steps of A TRUTH, using awareness and taking responsibility for your part in this situation, you can start to climb off the triangle. You have to begin by analysing what your needs are and slowly hand back some responsibility to those around you.

EXERCISE 8
WHAT CAN I DELEGATE?

Think of the top five jobs you do every day, either at home or work sometimes many times a day, that both bug you the most and you also feel must be done.

Think about what they mean to you when they are done well.

An example might be:

I like to keep on top of my washing and ironing. By not letting it pile up and become a mountain of clean unironed clothes, I can get my kids dressed quickly and easily, always knowing where their clean clothes are, saving time for us to play and have fun.

It may feel strange to apply needs being met to a household task. However, when you look at the macro elements of juggling children, a house and maybe a job as well, simple household tasks not being done can seriously affect your equilibrium. Think about what happens and how your needs are affected when jobs are not done.

My frustration at not being able to find the girls' school socks, for them to be buried at the bottom of PE bags for the last week, means I end up running late, getting frustrated, feeling sad at letting myself and my kids down.

Yes, it's just clean socks, but the inner critic of a caretaker can turn it into a real nail in the coffin of self-esteem and self-confidence.

From here, work out what need you meet by getting tasks done by someone else.

From understanding your need, start to understand and have awareness of what the outcome of a job being done to your standards means to you.

I need the dishwasher emptied before bed, as I have a need for a calm, efficient breakfast for the family, to get out in time for the school run, allowing my family to have time to talk about our day ahead.

Then start to diffuse its importance in the broader context of having someone else do it sometimes.

If the dishwasher was not emptied to my standard, I could finish it as I make tea later in the day, grateful that the person who emptied it had an intention to help, and that I want to encourage and support that intention to meet my need for support.

By the way, this doesn't mean that you can't share with the other person that you would like them to do it differently in the future, but coming from a grateful and calmer disposition means that your request for the task to be done differently might be better received and acted on.

Now think about which tasks you could start to relinquish and share with the people around you who could help.

But do not, having read this, show everyone the triangle and announce with conviction: "Things are going to change around here!" You might freak everyone out!

WARNING! If you have been cycling around the drama triangle for a while, maybe for years, remember that those around you could be experiencing serious emotional baggage, fear and resentment of change, as they may have battled to help many times and have been struck down by your reactions to their efforts. So acknowledge their fears and explain that you are trying to let go of your need to control how things are done, and accept their support with gratitude.

Learn to let go of your need for particular outcomes. Release a task that you can explain fully and well and once they have done it, thank them and leave it just as they have. (Unless it causes danger to human life, of course.)

An example would be giving your partner the job of making tea for the family in two days' time, letting them plan, shop for and make the meal. Do not tell them what is in the fridge, what you all had for lunch, how many portions of fruit the kids have had or what you want cooked. Let them roll with it. You will be amazed what others can contribute when given half a chance.

"ME" TIME – IT'S ESSENTIAL, NOT A LUXURY

The need for love and closeness is more obvious to people than the need for separateness. Many of us fill our daily lives with fulfilling the demands of parental, social, professional and personal roles. One thing we often forget as mums is that all human beings also have a need for separateness, a time to regain our internal integrity and balance, on our own.

For me that can be anything from reading my book at the local pub and having a glass of Buck's Fizz, a coffee at the coffee shop or a meditation on the beach, or just a deep bubble bath when the kids are in bed, each bringing a different type of sanity to my mind.

Work out what would give you "me" time, a break from having to fulfil anyone else's needs, and find a way, even if it is only once a month, to do what will regain your mental peace.

WHAT'S THE STORY?

Alex has taken her 6-year-old daughter Mia to the local farm park for the day. They are having a girls' day all to themselves. They start off feeding lambs from bottles and then go to the household pets corner and spend an hour petting rabbits and guinea pigs. As a special treat, they go through to the café for lunch and Alex offers Mia whatever she wants to have on the menu. She chooses fish fingers and chips for her main course and a bag of homemade cookies for her pudding. She decides to save her cookies for later, to eat next to the duck pond in the sun, with her mum.

Alex and Mia enjoy a lovely few hours on pony rides and looking at the animals, then settle down next to the duck pond to eat the cookies on one of the picnic tables. It's very busy so they have to share the table with another family. Mia opens the bag of cookies, takes one out and bites into it with glee. Then to her and her mum's surprise, the dad from the other family, a Japanese gentleman, puts his hand into the bag and takes out one of the cookies and gives it to his son. Alex pointedly takes out a cookie, showing the man that these are their cookies and not for public consumption. She is vaguely thinking that the gentleman must be on holiday here and have a slight misunderstanding of British culture, and she gives the cookie to Mia, moves the bag closer to them, and smiles and nods at the dad, trying to make her point clear.

To her shock, the man leans across, picks up the bag and takes a cookie out for himself.

Mia bursts into tears, causing the man to look perplexed. He grabs his son by the hand and walks away.

What do you think? What would you have done in that situation? Would you have said anything to the man?

The day blighted, a confused and slightly angry Alex gets back to the house that evening and, while recounting the tale to her partner, unpacks the bag they had taken to the farm, pulling out their unopened bag of homemade cookies.

It is an identical bag to the cookies they were eating at the table, the ones that belonged to the Japanese dad.

Does this change your thoughts about the Japanese man?

Have your feelings for him changed now?

How many times do you have thoughts and feelings about something, somebody or a situation, only to discover later or on reflection that the circumstances you believed had triggered those thoughts and feelings had been incorrect?

How often have those feelings and unmet needs caused you to act in a way that on reflection you feel was inappropriate or unfair?

One thing we need to recognise is that our thoughts do not always come from reality. Does that matter?

Our thoughts, feelings and needs are all harmless. They have no impact on us or others until we start to believe them and act on them as if they were true or real.

A belief is a thought that we have been attaching feelings to, often for years. I'm going to ask you to look at your thoughts and beliefs as:

A cartoon
A mental movie
Or a fictional story

Our mind creates this movie or story, sometimes several times a day, and then accepts it as real.

Let me tell you about Sophie, one evening in October.

Her two boys had colds; they were snotty, grumpy, with persistent, irritating coughs. Her husband had an early flight the next morning and needed to be up at 4 a.m. to get to the airport on time. Despite also having a busy day ahead, Sophie offered to look after both the boys through the night and sleep in the spare room, so her husband would have the minimum of disruption.

She finally settled two very snuffly, sad little boys at about 11 p.m. and, in an effort to minimise disruption, tiptoed along the dark landing to the spare room without turning on the light. She brushed her teeth and changed in the bathroom, in the dark, and then inched her way across to the spare bedroom. Crack! She stubbed her toe on something hard and cold. Hopping around in the dark, she then fell over the obstacle and landed hard on her arm, shouting out with pain.

Eyes closed and trying desperately to be quiet, she turned on the light, only to see that the assailant in the dark was her husband's half-packed suitcase, left right in the middle of the landing, blocking the door to the spare room.

In psychological terms, what has happened to Sophie is that she has encountered a first-level stressor: an obstacle, event or experience in life from which she has experienced a consequence.

Did she therefore take a deep breath, choose her response with a Zen-like calm, quietly climb into bed and decide to tell her husband when he got back that her need for safety and non-sore toes had not been met and could he please not leave his suitcase on the landing in the future?

Did she heck! She chose a very different response.

Her first thought was: "What the hell was he doing leaving the suitcase in the middle of the floor? How stupid! How could he be so inconsiderate?"

Her thoughts spiralled up through the levels of stressors of all the past "crimes" her husband had committed until she was furious: "And I was being so considerate, he is always inconsiderate, he never thinks about me, how could he do this to me? He is unbelievable, expecting me to make all these sacrifices for him and he swans off..."

Rather than going to bed, nursing her toe and having a calm-ish discussion with her husband on his return, her thoughts, feelings and unmet needs led her to – yes, you guessed it – storm into their bedroom, slamming on the light and shouting at her husband: "What the hell did you think you were doing? You inconsiderate...!"

You can imagine the rest. This of course culminated in their raised voices waking both poorly boys and full-scale pandemonium erupting.

The stressor theory is examined and evaluated in Buddhism, but unless you live in isolation in a monastery for 40 years and never work or become a mum, you cannot avoid first-level stressors. Painful events, challenges, actions and experiences will happen to you, this is inevitable, unchangeable, life. However, as Buddha said:

Pain is inevitable   *Suffering is optional*

In other words, the stresses will happen, but you and you alone choose whether you respond to them by increasing your level of suffering. Within seconds, Sophie went from one painful event to a journey of mental escalation, taking her to a place that could only bring additional suffering. She wrote a story in her head, linking past unmet needs, feelings and resentments into the suitcase crime and creating a pool of thoughts and emotions, which burst out at her husband.

So where do the initial stressor and its impact stop and a story start? Let me tell you about my first day back at work.

I had put everything in place for going back to work: spent three months organising everything to the *n*th degree, childcare sorted, long, repetitive discussions with my 3 year old about Mummy going back to work, hours spent building security in my 9 month old by responding to every whimper and cry, working from the evidence that doing this early on builds self-esteem and security. That combined with nine months of shush-shushing, patting and pick-up/put-down sleep training, all to no avail, meaning I still never got to sleep for longer than three hours at a time.

Yet the first day comes, and 15 minutes before I have to leave I get baby and toddler Lego out and decide to spend quality time building towers with my boys. Two seconds in and the single yellow, one-bump square with a dog on becomes the only block either of my sons wants. After three rounds of snatching and a refusal on either side to accept any other block, I have two boys in tantruming, whole-body-consuming, very loud, hysterical tears.

My eldest is bereft that not only will Mummy not let him have the only block ever worth having in the whole entire world, she is also leaving him, seemingly never to return. There are breathless pleas of "Don't leave me!" "Oh and *please* may I have my block" and "I said please!" (When did him finally learning to say "please" stop being polite and become the same as a demand, because if he said it with a please surely it must happen?) My youngest is unaware of my imminent defection and yet, totally bereft that the said brick has been put away out of sight, is banging his head rhythmically on the floor as he screams. And I have to hand over to the nanny and walk away...

83

I climb into my car, smiling and waving at my devastated boys, only to stop as soon as I am out of view to burst into tears.

Did I calmly take a deep breath, knowing that my boys were safe and cared for and would be fine, and concentrate on my exciting, nerve-racking day ahead? Of course not, I wrote my mental story and my stressors started building.

My story read like this:

"My poor babies, they need their Mummy. A good mum should be at home with her children. God, I'm a terrible mum! I should be there for them, I shouldn't be going back to work. We should scrimp and save more, buy less, economise, tighten our belts, so I can stay home. I should be stronger, a better mum, and stay home making savings another way. Why can't I be satisfied with being a full-time mum, why was it not enough? I'm such a failure, I can't even get right something a woman is born to be.

"My poor boys, what damage am I doing to them? They will be sad and lonely today, in fact they will be psychologically scarred for life with the feelings of abandonment, loneliness, separation, desolation... They will fail at school, not form friendships, never have functional, happy, satisfying relationships, they will drift from heartbreak to heartbreak and it's all my fault..."

You get the idea! I created a complex story which in turn produced totally unresourceful, useless and unfounded thoughts and feelings that I have no idea or evidence my boys are experiencing, creating in myself feelings of shame, guilt, pain and sadness. In reality I know they probably are not experiencing a fraction of those emotions, and they are going to be far happier with a fulfilled, stimulated working mum four days a week, than an exhausted, slightly bored and definitely bordering on mildly insane mum seven days a week.

The story we write and our subsequent thoughts and feelings have an impact on how we behave, and become visible to the rest of the world. Our story creates the way we interact and has a real impact on others and ourselves.

Looking back at Sophie, by the time her husband had put the light on, in her thoughts he had gone from a supportive, hard-working husband requiring consideration and sleep to a selfish, uncaring, thoughtless husband requiring anger. Her response stemming from her stressful thoughts and feelings about him meant that she lost her temper and lambasted him. On reflection, the reality of the situation was very different.

All mums who build a story about our "poor" children and imagine that we "abandon them" carry around a heavy weight of guilt, shame and disappointment in ourselves, which will reflect in everything we say and do.

One small note I would like to add here before we move on is that I am not advocating that we rewrite our perception of reality to create a picture that always looks positive and rosy. A world viewed through rose-tinted spectacles is no nearer to reality than one painted black through guilt or shame. I am starting to introduce the concept of living with our life and the reality of what it is without any bias.

MINDSET IN A MINUTE
THOUGHTS AND FEELINGS

Don't assume that your thoughts are real or true. They can grow from painful, stressful or challenging events in your past and they are often biased, exaggerated and 9 times out of 10 false. You need to start examining your thoughts as they create your actions.

Thoughts, feelings and emotions are our body's signals and messengers to us. We need to start hearing, acknowledging and releasing them. Feelings buried alive will ALWAYS resurface, often just when we least expect them and normally very unresourcefully.

When we are in a "bad mood" we are snappy, frustrated and irrational. Start to ask why. Start to release the emotions that are leaking out in your behaviour, often arising from events that happened long before your mood.

Acknowledging that no one else makes us think or feel anything, they just create a stimulus, allows us to start managing how we react to each life event.

Pain is inevitable   Stress is optional

Painful, hurtful, sad, uncontrollable events will happen, but by creating a story of suffering from each event we prolong, amplify and exaggerate the negative effects. By deconstructing our stories we can see each event in isolation and put our pain to rest.

We all have inherent, physiological and psychological needs. When our needs are continually ignored, negated, or deprioritised, we start to suffer. Begin to analyse, understand and acknowledge your needs, then where possible start to meet them.

Are you continuously caretaking and controlling those around you? Redoing things they have done and getting frustrated at their inability to get things right? Setting them tasks with the nth degree of detail?

Do you carry a backpack full of resentment and every once in a while explode at others' inability to get things right? Do you occasionally burst, airing months of frustration and vitriol in the space of two minutes, only to be overcome five minutes later with remiss and regret at the depth of your venom? You are stuck in the drama triangle.

Learn how to escape today. Start to trust others, release and reduce your levels of control, let go, delegate and allow others to help.

Believe me, if you start to let people they will help!

Pain is inevitable, we have no choice about it. Suffering is optional and we always have a choice about how we respond.

CHAPTER 3

LIVING IN REALITY

Your goals, minus your doubts, equal your reality.
—**Ralph Marston**

So, on our journey to A TRUTH we've gained some self-awareness and begun to get to grips with our thoughts and feelings. Now I am going to ask you to look more closely at the stories you are creating and to begin to analyse when you are acting on a story rather than on reality.

HOW DO I KNOW IF I'M LIVING IN A FAIRYTALE?

With every new event or context we encounter, an old story, from our childhood, previous relationships, or jobs, fertility challenges, painful experiences – the list is endless – can come to the surface. We build beliefs and views of the world and the people within it very early and seek evidence throughout our lives to support the stories we have created. So when we try to navigate and detect the truth of a situation from within a story, we can face many challenges.

Let me explain what I mean.

Alison, a new first-time mum, had built a successful life. She loves her work and had contributed greatly in her field, and believed she would continue to, she had planned her pregnancy and birth in the finest detail and was really looking forward to being a mum. She had grown up in a family with strong, intelligent, robust parents and siblings and was confident that family

LOVE YOU MUM

life would be a wonderful experience. Her story was written on an internal picture that babies were fun, sweet, cuddly, welcome additions to a family. When her daughter spent the first three weeks of her life screaming, not latching on, vomiting and not sleeping, Alison sought help.

All mums experience challenges with each new baby, of course. They have to learn how to meet their needs, and calming the baby while taking care of themselves and healing is truly hard.

However, Alison was also fighting her story of what she believed having and caring for a new baby should be like: fun, intimate, nurturing and affectionate. When we analysed her story, this allowed her to see that the first stressor of a new baby was real, but that her frustration, disappointment, disapproval and anger were all arising from a story she had mentally written of how her daughter would/should be based on zero facts.

When she was able to leave her story behind, she started to see her daughter for the normal, grouchy, crying, beautiful child she was and to see motherhood from a different perspective.

WHAT IF IT'S A HORROR STORY?

As with all analysis of our emotional and mental capacity – our thoughts, feelings and emotions – when we start to analyse where our feelings are based we may find areas of belief or stories that come from a memory or event that is very painful, sad or tragic. In this chapter I am going to be running through some techniques for dissecting, interpreting and dissolving stories. What I am not able to do is sit with you as you do this. So be kind to yourself, and talk things over with your friends if you're working through any stories or beliefs arising from events or memories that are causing you extensive pain.

Julie's dad had divorced her mother, leaving the family home, when she was a young teenager. She had put on weight in the few months before he left. Blaming herself for his departure, Julie had built a story in her mind creating strong beliefs that important people leave if you put on weight. As a mum herself she struggled throughout her pregnancy and the months following as breastfeeding caused her to gain and retain weight, creating fears that her partner would leave her. She was wracked with guilt about eating for the health of her child and herself yet trying to remain slim to keep her husband, never realising that her actions were caused by a story created from childhood. She became cold and off-hand with her husband, anger building from her assumption of his feelings of disgust towards her, and her own disgust at her extra weight.

When we analysed her story and saw the truth behind her fears, we discovered that she was unable to rewrite her deeper beliefs without some counselling about her feelings of loss and self-blame around her father leaving.

After a few weeks of professional support, she was able to talk openly to her partner and share with him her fears about his feelings towards her weight (he had no negative feelings about her shape at all) and also to relax and enjoy feeding her baby.

As I said before, the stories we create are not all negative. Nevertheless, it is essential that you examine your own stories to separate out reality and build your awareness of whether the feelings and behaviours you are displaying to others are fair and appropriate.

THE LANGUAGE OF STORIES

I am frequently asked how we can know whether we are creating a story about an event or even within a conversation with someone. I have one very simple way of identifying this. The first place to start dissecting stories is to examine the language you are using.

Do any of the following words appear in your thoughts or words?

He/she/I/they...   never, always, should, should not...

                        is/are bad, good, stupid...

                        is/are too lazy, strict, thin...

These words are all centred on having made a judgement, formed an opinion, something that has your interpretation, your beliefs and your viewpoint attached.

As brilliant as you may think your opinion is, it is always biased. It is only *your* view... sorry!

Whenever you place a judgemental word on a person or an action, you are not thinking, feeling or acting from unbiased reality, you are creating a judgement or story from your view of the world according to you, and acting accordingly.

Looking back at Sophie in the interlude, when she stubbed her toe she quickly moved from the singular event her husband had helped to create to accusing him of never thinking of her and always being selfish. Therefore the level of her anger with him compounded as she created a belief that it was not a one-off situation but a list of crimes fitting the description. When analysing this later, Sophie was very clear that her husband often did very supportive and selfless acts to help her and that this misdemeanour was in fact in the minority.

I am not advocating that you stop having opinions or beliefs, I am discussing whether your judgement or labelling of others or yourself is causing you to act in a way towards others, yourself or an event that is not rational and in proportion with reality.

GUILTY AGAIN

In my experience, nine times out of ten the guilt mums seem to feel comes from a basis of either should or should not, sometimes both.

More than any other phrase (except perhaps "I'm exhausted!"), I hear mums say: "I **should** have done that better, I **shouldn't** have shouted at my baby."

Their guilt and subsequent sadness, shame, regret, anger and disappointment come from a story called "I **should** have handled that better, I **should** not have done that, I feel so bad that I did or didn't do what I **should** have done. Or I **should** have achieved more..."

What is the **should** based on?

It comes from a story you have within your mind of what a good mother, a kind person, a rational human being should be and you are comparing yourself to that judgement.

Mary was consumed with guilt surrounding her son's reading ability. She had had discussions with the school about him being slightly behind the expected ability level for reading and spelling. Instead of focusing on a school system that was labelling her completely normal, capable, bright young son, she wrote a mental story about her faults as a mum and his faults for not being as good as he should be. She was critical and hard on him for not working hard enough, not studying when she told him to and not focusing on this crucial task in learning for life. (He was 6.)

This was her second child and she created a judgemental story that she had spent less time than she should have reading to him one on one as a young child; she now worked and had not always had time to have a bedtime story as she had with his elder sibling. She told herself she should have made it a priority to look at spellings, despite working and being heavily pregnant with her third child. She concluded that she had let her son down, failing in her role as a mum.

So she didn't only create a story about what she should have done, she also built guilt and further stories about how she was not treating and caring for her children equally.

When Mary and I looked for the reality and facts behind her stories and allowed the feelings caused by the stories to fade, she was able to support her son with his reading from a far more rational place – including apologising to him for her harsh comments following parents' evening at school.

EXERCISE 9
WHY ARE YOU GUILTY?

Think back to the last time you felt guilty about something.

♡ What thoughts/story sat behind the guilt?

♡ Was the guilt based on the reality and facts of the situation?

♡ Was the guilt based on a comparison with a judgement, label or assumption about what the outcome/behaviour/action should have been?

Now try doing the same exercise for the last time you felt angry, out of control or sad. Run through the same questions: were your feelings coming from facts or your story attached to the facts?

BUT IT'S TRUE!

You may be convinced that the story you have created for yourself is true. Without going into a tremendous amount of detail about how we psychologically filter facts to make the evidence support our stories, I have simplified and adapted two pieces of research in this area. The first is called the "ladder of inference".

In the early 1970s two psychologists, Donald Schon and Chris Argyris, developed a psychological model of how we observe facts and then produce assumptions to make sense of what we have observed. From those assumptions we construct conclusions, stories and feelings, and we behave according to these.

Below is an adapted version of Argyris and Schon's model.

Let's look at the ladder in action.

Sally got together with five other mums every Tuesday morning. They first met at antenatal classes and had their children within days of each other. Over the course of these coffee shop gatherings, Sally had noticed that Devon, one of the more confident mums, would get up, go to the loo, get another drink or change her baby whenever Sally was talking. On one particular Tuesday, not only had Devon got up twice, as Sally had talked about her mother-in-law's visit that weekend, Devon had loudly and very obviously yawned.

Sally felt that Devon didn't value or respect her and was quite willing to show this publically. To her, Devon's actions were demonstrating her lack of approval of the way Sally was parenting, which was very different from the older mum. Sally started to distrust Devon. Over the weeks Sally began to believe her to be divisive within the group of mums and responsible for the sense of discomfort that was starting to pervade their meetings. She shared with other mums on occasions when Devon was not there the evidence she had collected and started to rally their opinions and support for her story.

What is scary is just how fast we climb up our ladder and make these inferences or assumptions and that we act on them because we feel they are true. Why do they feel so real? The story we create, rather than what has actually taken place, magnifies the feelings we are having about the situation.

Initially Sally is frustrated when Devon goes to the loo when she is speaking, but that frustration turns into anger and deep suspicion when the assumption/story is formed that her intention behind going to the loo is based on disrespecting or undermining Sally's standing in the group.

Having written this story, Sally proceeded to find all the observable evidence she needed to prove to the others what she believed Devon was doing – and of course she found it. She believed that she was basing her story on facts and felt justified about her subsequent actions. In other words, her story and the assumptions she had in her mind became the truth.

What is really sad about this model is that once Sally had climbed up her ladder and started bad mouthing Devon to the others, the chances were that Devon would hear of it. Devon would then start to act defensively around Sally, only reinforcing her beliefs.

So in essence Sally had two observable facts: Devon leaving the group when she was talking and Devon yawning while she was sharing an experience. These two pieces of observable data were expanded into a story called "Devon disapproves of me, Devon will turn these new friends against me, and Devon is not to be trusted."

Until we analysed the facts again:

♡ Did Devon ever get up when others were talking?

♡ Did Devon ever reinforce or support Sally in her opinions or needs?

♡ Did Devon have a true and justified reason for yawning?

Once Sally had become aware of her ladder and the story she had created, she had the opportunity to break free from her biased view. With hindsight, she realised that Devon had done all of those things. In fact, once she came back down her ladder she was amazed to see how quickly her perceptions changed, especially three weeks later when Devon, who had been under significant stress, broke down in tears and shared that she was dealing with a daughter who had severe stomach problems and actually was leaving the group frequently to look after her. She was also suffering from severe postnatal depression, causing her need to distance herself from some of their conversation that caused her to feel inadequate or tearful. She was coping with medication that left her exhausted and drained. Sally now only felt compassion where before there had been anger and contempt.

To evaluate the reality behind a story, you need to establish the full original facts. The easiest way to do this – to eliminate the bias, judgement, opinion and interpretation and only take the observable facts – is only to evaluate the things that a video camera would pick up. Place no opinion or label on them, just let them stand alone.

In this example:

♡ Devon did get up a few times when Sally was talking.
♡ Devon did once yawn while Sally was talking.
♡ Devon got up when the others were talking.
♡ Devon yawned all the time.
♡ Devon often supported Sally's words and displayed sympathy.

The last three facts were ones that Sally had deleted from her view as they did not support her initial assumptions.

EXERCISE 10
LOOK AT THE EVIDENCE

Look back at the stories you had created the last time you were angry or felt guilty. In retrospect, re-examine the evidence you compiled to support your beliefs:

♡ Had or have you formed any assumptions from the facts?

♡ Have you escalated those assumptions to a higher level of judgement or conclusion?

♡ Can you now see or remember evidence to disprove what you were thinking?

STAYING ON THE BOTTOM RUNG OF YOUR LADDER

One of the quickest ways to reduce your stress levels substantially every day is to start observing your ladder of inference and, through self-observation and self-awareness, stay on the bottom rung.

An example could be things being left on the floor: children's toys, shoes, coats, your partner's clothes, towels, the list is endless. Rather than making huge leaps up your ladder with inferences about the level of laziness and ignorance of those about you, just observe the facts as they stand.

As mad as it sounds, the facts may purely be: "My family have not yet learnt to pick up their things."

Then you can communicate with them from that place, not five steps up the ladder with angry proclamations about them treating you like a housekeeper and the house like a hotel. Simply start making requests of them to take the actions you need.

It may sound like you are letting them off the hook, but think about it: who is your getting angry really benefiting?

Is it you?
Is it them?

My belief is that it is benefiting no one. Getting angry from rung number 5 of your ladder just adds to your stress levels and wears you out.

So here's a quick stress-fix exercise.

EXERCISE 11
INSTANT STRESS RELIEF

Over the next week, become aware of the events or actions of others that are negatively affecting you.

Examples could be:

♡ Delivery people not turning up
♡ Washing machines or other appliances breaking down
  (I keep using this example, I seem to have a very poor track record with washing machines)
♡ Your partner forgetting something you've asked him to do
♡ Kids – well, kids being kids

When one of these events happens, stay very aware and remain at the bottom of your ladder, hold on to pure facts, accept them and act accordingly.

Believe me, when you're able to stay at the bottom of your ladder for about 70 per cent of the events that happen daily, you get a huge reduction in the amount of stress.

FIND THE REALITY – DECONSTRUCT YOUR STORY

When I argue with reality, I lose – but only 100% of the time. —**Byron Katie**

In her book *Loving What Is*, Byron Katie shares her very simple formula for examining and getting to the truth of a mental story. She has probably had more influence over my work and my life than any other practitioner, as I found this technique invaluable for dissecting the stories in my life.

She maintains that we only experience mental suffering when we argue with reality, with what is.

Right now, in the present moment, everything is as it is. Being angry, sad, frustrated, disappointed, scared or fed up will not change the facts, and will only bring you unnecessary suffering.

Right now, you may be tired, overweight, bored, suffering from cancer, desperate for another child, lonely or many other realities. Accepting now for what it is is the first step to ending the pain associated with your stories. It is where you are. If you feel anything other than acceptance, you are only feeling unnecessary pain.

Not accepting reality, or where we are right now, is where our "shoulds" come in again: I **should** be a better mum, my child **should** sleep at night, my partner **should** help more, I **should** have got that promotion, the sun **should** be shining, I **shouldn't** have this cold. These thoughts all want reality to be different from what it is. Where you are now can never be different to how it is. You can change your future, but not your now.

If you believe something should not have happened or be happening, it actually should, because it has or is. Accept it! No tears, anger, frustration or pain will change something that is. As horrific, heartbreaking, devastating, everyday or mundane the reality is, the truth is that any energy spent wishing it was not is wasted.

When I first encountered this concept, I worried that this way of thinking felt like submission, becoming weak, passive, losing goals and opinions. However, as soon as I started using the technique I found it invaluable in many aspects of my thinking every day.

I am not suggesting that you turn off or ignore your negative emotions. In many truly painful circumstances, emotions are your coping mechanism. Grief, pain, self-pity and sadness have essential psychological functions, but there is always a point where acceptance can allow you to move forward.

I have seen Byron Katie work with a mother whose son had committed suicide two years earlier. The mum was consumed with her pain and anger for her lost son. She said: "He should have talked to me, he should have asked for help, I should have been a better mother and known how low he was." Katie gently worked through her process and I watched this grief-stricken mum, in the space of five minutes, move to a place of acceptance that her son had decided to end his life. He had chosen not to ask for help, he had used his right to make his own decision and that was the reality. Nothing she felt or thought would change the facts.

She would still mourn the loss of her 15-year-old son, and yet she could now start to let herself off the hook, rewrite her story, her thoughts, feelings and behaviours, and accept the truth of what had happened.

Byron Katie's work is explained fully in *Loving What Is*. She also has many worksheets and examples on her website (www.thework.com) explaining how to dissect and enquire into your stories. In this book I am just going to share with you the first stage:

You have to look for the thought or story that is creating suffering.

> ## EXERCISE 12
> ## FIND THE REALITY
>
> Ask four questions of any thought that is causing you suffering:
>
> ♡ Is it true?
> ♡ Can you absolutely know that it is true?
> ♡ How do you react when you think that thought?
> ♡ Who would you be without the thought?

Here is one of the mums whose inter-fear-ance I shared earlier and her personal experience of using this technique.

> *My husband is incapable of noticing the mess he creates. He lives in a world where he believes he is helping and yet he is oblivious to the towels, empty mugs, shoes, shopping bags – the list is endless – that he discards randomly across the house. I'm not even sure he knows what our dishwasher and washing machine are for. God knows how he would cope with the kids if I ever got ill!*

First break down the situation to the first thought that is causing pain:

> *My husband is incapable of noticing the mess he creates.*

Is that thought true?

> *Yes, he is not stupid and yet he is totally oblivious to the mess.*

Often the first answer to this question while you are still reacting from your story is "yes". Ask yourself again, particularly if you are talking about the words or actions of another human being. Are you really able to know what is in their mind?

Can you absolutely know that your thought is true?

The only way to answer this truly is just to listen to yourself, not your story, not your pain but the truth.

> *No, he is not incapable of noticing the mess. At times he moans about it, gets frustrated at losing his keys, his phone, his book, so he does notice the mess.*

How do you react when you think your thought about his actions?

> *I feel angry, resentful, put upon, tired. I think he is selfish and lazy and just treats me like a doormat.*

Who would you be without the thought?

This is so important. You are not asking: How can I change this reality? or How can I speak to my husband? Just focus on your thought and what it is doing to you, the one part of this situation you have responsibility for and control over.

> *If I didn't have the thought that my husband is totally incapable of noticing the mess he creates, I would feel calmer. My husband is not currently noticing or clearing up the mess. That is how it is.*

The thought is a "**should**" arguing with "what is".

Having worked through the rest of her thoughts, this mum accepted that her husband, at present, is not meeting her need for support with the housework. She is experiencing many unresourceful feelings from thinking these thoughts about his support.

Once again, this does not mean that she does nothing to change the situation. She might well talk to her husband. The difference is that she accepts the reality: her husband is messy and will be messy until he isn't!

Her attempts to fight that and nag, as she has done for the last seven years, achieve nothing except pain and stress for her. Without her story, she can talk to her husband from a far more rational space.

By coming to terms and being more at peace with her situation, she does not yet have a husband who is any different, more supportive or meeting her needs. However, she is no longer consumed with negative feelings and the actions and behaviours towards her husband that they cause.

Later in the book I will talk you through how to start making clear requests to those around you to begin getting your needs met and honestly communicating your needs and expectations without unresourceful feelings leaking out. But taking control of the impact of your thoughts is the first step.

Let me share where this process changed my perspective as a mum. My story was that my 4-month-old son was lying in hospital with meningitis.

It is so unfair, why has my poor baby got meningitis?

Is that true?

Of course it is unfair that my innocent 4-month-old baby has contracted something that could kill him or leave him brain damaged, and it's causing him pain!

Can you absolutely know that is true?

Is it true that it is unfair? It feels unfair, but I guess I can't know if it is universally, truly unfair, as fairness is different for different people, it is subjective. So no, I cannot know for sure that that is true.

How do you react when you think that thought that it is so unfair?

The unfairness is making me feel angry, resentful and sad. I am angry that it is my son and that it is not fair. My anger is causing me to be snappy, bitter and aggressive to everyone, when in reality those around me are desperate to help, and I am biting their heads off.

Who would you be without the thought?

Without the thought that it is not fair, I am still sad, ter-rified for my boy, but less angry with the unjustness. I am still bereft and scared, but I am less angry and aggressive.

My son still had meningitis, there was still nothing I could do but give him love, but in the moment, having faced the reality of the thoughts that were bringing me pain and notic-ing that my behaviour was becoming unresourceful, it was making things worse for those around me, not better.

After dissecting my story, I was able to share my sad-ness, my terror and my vulnerability with my family and embrace their support for me as I supported my son. He is now a fit, healthy and totally recovered little boy.

Byron Katie goes on to discuss how to turn around thoughts that are bringing you pain, and takes you on a very simple but comprehensive journey through the pain that your argument with reality can produce. This is a process that I totally endorse and recommend, but I am leaving that for your personal journey beyond reading this book. My thanks to Byron Katie and her organisation for their permission to use this material in my book.

I AM ONLY HUMAN, GILL – GIVE ME A BREAK!

I do know that applying logic at times of stress is hard to do, often impossible.

With this process and all the others in this book, I am not asking you to punish yourself in the midst of a painful, stressful situation or when you feel you may have reacted in a way you wish you hadn't. We can be too hard on ourselves. None of the work in this book is designed to arm you with more ammunition to attack yourself about how terrible a job you're doing. (Watch out for the FAB response later in the book for tips on how to improve your ability to respond.)

But it is important to appreciate that when you are able to be self-aware about the potential negative consequences of thoughts you are having, you can start to amend the way you react and choose a response that brings you peace with yourself.

The last few chapters have examined what could be behind the inter-fear-ances that are preventing your behaviour and actions above the water line from being what you want them to be. By assessing what you are thinking, how you are feeling and the needs beneath that feeling, and then checking that the needs and feelings are based on reality, not a story, you are starting to take responsibility for understanding why you are acting in the way you are.

I would love to tell you that this day-to-day, hour-to-hour, thought-to-thought process becomes second nature and you can instantly choose a response to a stressful event – but I can't. This is a lifetime journey for me and everyone else I know who has encountered this work. Each new scenario in your life could tap into new stories, new beliefs formed and stored long before the event, and the process requires your attention. For as long as you choose to select your response, for as long as you choose to be the person you have always wanted to be, you will keep encountering new challenges and travelling through the steps of A TRUTH all over again.

I have been practising this and other techniques for a number of years and my friends and family will all agree that I still sometimes react in a way that brings pain to others – and I always will. I forgive myself and accept that in myself, as I know I will keep on trying.

BIRTH STORIES

Human beings are programmed to continually develop and grow, but I believe we often negate responsibility for creating our own outcomes, actually finding the stories we have created a comfort or an excuse for our behaviour and actions.

I know I run the risk of alienating some readers with this discussion, but one of the most obvious examples for me is our childbirth stories, which we use for several potential reasons.

When I became pregnant for the first time, I was suddenly hooked into one of the greatest story books of all time: the painful birth story. My wonderful, bright, caring friends, strangers in a queue, my relatives and my midwife, all seemed to take apparent pleasure – "It's important you know", "I'd hate to lie to you" – in sharing with me graphic and horrific birth stories.

Obviously, the biology of getting an 8lb baby out of a hole occasionally (tired mum!) used for a far smaller inhabitant is going to be physically challenging. But why do we need to dissect and embellish the extent of the pain for our newly pregnant friends? Many pregnant women are terrified of giving birth having heard from others how horrific it can be.

And when we do experience a traumatic, excruciating birth, witnessed and shared with a traumatised, eternally grateful partner, we suddenly have the greatest get-out-of-jail card known to womankind. Mediators call this a trump card. It is a statement of fact delivered in a discussion that cannot be bettered or even equalled by a man:

How can you say that? I gave birth to our child for you!

We use this as a longlasting excuse for many things, from not being ready to have sex (far easier than discussing the real feelings we have about resuming a physical relationship), to starting fitness regimes, dieting, or even just making a cup of tea.

I have also met countless fathers whose level of admiration and awe for their wife's perceived battle and courage in childbirth lasted long after their child's first birthday, something the women both relished and fully utilised.

Whatever our experience of giving birth, it is a wholly natural, frequently repeated event. Some of us do carry the experience with us for the rest of our lives, but what do we gain by terrifying our friends or using our partner's fear and awe to gain Brownie points or an exaggerated need for support or reward?

Using a story for a personal outcome is nothing but manipulation. But let's be honest, labelling or judgement stories can also, often completely unconsciously, make us feel better or worse about ourselves (at least temporarily).

When we look at another mum and either unconsciously or knowingly label them, we label ourselves by comparison. Either we create a story of perfection, ascribing organised, proactive and real "yummy mummy" status to another mum, and berating ourselves for not being as organised, creative or slim, with children who are not as tidy/creative/bright as hers, often based on nothing but an assumptive story. Alternatively we watch a mum with two dirty-faced, misbehaving, noisy children (yes, they are mine) and, consciously or not, judge her a failure in a way that brings us a certain satisfaction.

Equally divisive are the stories of suffering we share, the competition to have had the least sleep, the worst experience of a crying child, tantrums, teenage angst or lack of support from our partner. We get into a competition of one-upmanship about who is having the worst experience of mothering. But all these stories are almost always the result of us being unable to analyse and interpret what we need, and creating, totally unconsciously, a story to make us feel better.

A mum who needs positive support for a battered self-image or lack of self-worth may find it easier to make her level of suffering appear insurmountable and gain respect from that, rather than just acknowledging in herself her need for reassurance and morale boosting.

A mum frustrated at her inability to start a fitness or diet regime may believe that her level of stress and lack of sleep because of her "difficult" child excuses her lack of action and the failings she believes she has.

I am by no means innocent: I have used judgement, gossip, one-upmanship and excuses to help me feel better or to meet my needs, but I now know that the person I was when believing those stories is not a me I like very much, and certainly not the kind of mum I want my children to see.

It is your call, your intuition to assess, your own place to analyse whether you are gaining anything from stories and judgements you are making of others, your children, your partner or yourself. Hardest of all, only you can know if you have a story that is helping you to make an excuse not to move forward.

As you increase your self-awareness through the exercises in this book, and you start to observe and dissect your stories, keep yourself in check as to whether any of the stories are serving a particular purpose for you.

You may have strong feelings about my opinions; I'm always really interested to hear what other mums think. Drop me a line at the website and share with me how this makes you feel.

MINDSET IN A MINUTE
LIVING IN REALITY

Start to turn off guilt, realise that judgements are the root of all guilt, shame and regret.

Become aware of and turn off: I should have, I always, I never...

Start to see the truth of each event with clarity, isolation and without judgement.

We can all start to mentally collect evidence to support our point of view, excluding and ignoring all the evidence to support the contrary. We climb up a ladder of inference or assumption, linking random pieces of a jigsaw and leaving the picture incomplete. This causes us to form views, opinions and judgements of others based on pure bias, not the whole truth.

Follow this path to instant stress relief, when a negative event affects you, consciously stay aware of your mental state and remain on the bottom rung of your ladder, hold on to the pure facts, accept them and act accordingly.

Deconstruct the stories you are creating about yourself, others and stressful situations. Start to ask yourself "Is that true?" about any thoughts, assumptions, accusations or anger you have towards others.

Begin to ask yourself whether your stories are supporting your excuses, reinforcing your denial of painful truths, or just temporarily making you feel better about yourself? Are they creating pain for others or reducing them to judgemental labels or boxes?

CHAPTER 4

UNDERSTANDING WHO YOU ARE

I am not a person who has yet been brave enough to step off my treadmill and travel the world to "find" myself. Through all my years of teaching and learning personal development, I have worked, learnt in and traversed the professional arena. Have I found me? Who knows? What I have definitely found is the knowledge that the only person I can change, or have any right to change, is me. So if I have areas of my life, professional or personal, with my family or my friends, that I am unhappy with, only I can find and adapt what has to happen for me to be happier.

I can't and don't need to understand what makes you happy, but I know that you do!

I also believe that many of the traits that make us who we are, formed from our own unique genetics, socialisation and choices, are with us for life. They will differ depending on the situation we find ourselves in. We can choose our responses to situations, but the reality is, we are who our life and our experiences have made us. Therefore it is useful to know who we are, as best we can, so we can know and understand who we are spending the rest of our life with.

This part of A TRUTH – understanding – looks at who you are and enables you, with curiosity and a sense of acceptance, to understand the reality that is you.

UNDERSTANDING WHAT YOU VALUE

Whether we are consciously aware of them or not, every individual has a core set of personal values. Values are our judgements about what is important in life. To live a life misaligned from your inherent values would cause you to lose your personal identity and your sense of worth. Your values are your internal benchmark of what is good, beneficial, important, useful, beautiful, desirable, appropriate – to you. These are the foundational beliefs that make you *you*.

If I were to quickly ask you what are your basic, fundamental values, could you tell me?

Put on the spot, many people reel off a list of what they believe their values should be: honesty, integrity, spirituality, goodness, fun etc. Only when pressed do they request time and space to really think about their underpinning values.

That is exactly what I am going to ask you to do now.

EXERCISE 13
WHAT ARE YOUR VALUES?

Create a list of the ten most important values to you, either from the list opposite or from your own thinking.

1	6
2	7
3	8
4	9
5	10

Prioritise those values from 1–10, with the most important to you being number 1.

Create a top three based on those scores.

1

2

3

Accomplishment, success
Accountability
Accuracy
Adventure
All for one & one for all
Beauty
Calm, quietude, peace
Challenge
Change
Cleanliness, orderliness
Collaboration
Commitment
Communication
Community
Competence
Competition
Concern for others
Connection
Content over form
Continuous improvement
Cooperation
Coordination
Creativity
Customer satisfaction
Decisiveness
Delight of being, joy
Democracy
Discipline
Discovery
Diversity
Ease of use
Efficiency
Equality
Excellence

Fairness
Faith
Faithfulness
Family
Family feeling
Flair
Freedom
Friendship
Fun
Global view
Goodwill
Goodness
Gratitude
Hard work
Harmony
Honesty
Honour
Improvement
Independence
Individuality
Inner peace, calm, quietude
Innovation
Integrity
Intensity
Justice
Knowledge
Leadership
Love, romance
Loyalty
Maximum utilisation
(of time, resources)
Meaning
Merit
Money

Openness
Patriotism
Peace, non-violence
Perfection
Personal growth
Pleasure
Power
Practicality
Preservation
Privacy
Progress
Prosperity, wealth
Punctuality
Quality of work
Regularity
Reliability
Resourcefulness
Respect for others
Responsiveness
Results orientation
Rule of law
Safety
Satisfying others
Security
Self-giving

Self-reliance
Self-thinking
Service (to others, society)
Simplicity
Skill
Solving problems
Speed
Spirit in life (using)
Stability
Standardisation
Status
Strength
Succeed, a will to
Success, achievement
Systematisation
Teamwork
Timeliness
Tolerance
Tradition
Tranquillity
Trust
Truth
Unity
Variety
Wisdom

This very simple exercise will highlight for you the values you believe to be the core of who you are, who you want to be.

EXERCISE 14
HOW DO YOU LIVE YOUR VALUES?

Take your three chosen values and write each at the top of a different piece of A4 paper.

Then under each value, write down each activity you do either daily or weekly that would demonstrate that value in your daily life.

(Warning: don't list what you think you *should* be doing, but what you actually *are* doing.)

If your three pages are full of activities, you can be happy that you are living and reinforcing your values in your life today.

If (as most people do) you find you can't write more than a couple of things, then it is likely that your current behaviours are not in line with what you value.

I have my three most important values on the notice-board in my kitchen, attached to a picture that makes me smile every time I look at it. It is a constant reminder of what is important to me. It is a reminder I associate with happiness and fun, not a standard to berate or punish myself against, just a gentle nudge not to take life too seriously (one of my values).

Another additional exercise that can be fun as your children get older and would like a say in family matters is that you and your family sit down and try the next exercise.

EXERCISE 15
FAMILY VALUES

If your children are young, create a family set of values between you and your partner; if your children are old enough, create your core values list as a group.

With a sense of fun, talk about why each of these values is important to you and why you want them as core to your lives together. Create a list of about 5, incorporating those that are fundamental to each member of the family.

My 3 year old currently thinks that driving a lorry is tanta-mount to eternal peace in his world, so right now, lorry driving is an aspirational value in our house!

One thing that will not work is if you pin up your list, having had a good discussion, and then ignore it. Ensure you know what living your values would look like by writing down some examples of the actions, behaviours and forms of communica-tion you can use to live out and embody them.

For each of the values you have chosen, identify specific things you do or can do to demonstrate that value. Write them down and share them with your family and friends.

Not only does this let you feel you are living the way you want, it gives clear identification to those who care about you of how they can meet your value-based needs (something, believe it or not, that those who care about you will truly want to do).

As with all the exercises in this book and the behaviours they create within you, your child or children will learn, grow and interpret their world through watching the way you act. Your actions will always speak louder than words, so live and behave according to your values, as well as talking about them.

UNDERSTANDING YOURSELF

The next section is going to ask you to look at yourself and at areas that you may perceive to be negative. It may invoke feelings of fear, anger, indignation or just dislike as you read them, both towards me and maybe yourself. I am happy to take the risk (easy for me to say, I know) – are you?

Intuitively you may read a section and know whole-heartedly that it does not apply to you. I would suggest that you still read and acknowledge it as another mum's challenge and move on. Be aware that the stronger the negative reaction you have to any particular idea and subsequent exercises, the more relevant it may actually be for you. The louder I hear someone proclaim they are "not" something, the more it turns out they are.

We often dislike, hate and revile the parts of others that deep down we know we have as a part of us. We have just created coping or avoidance patterns to avoid acknowledging them.

When you read the next few sections, take a deep breath, push aside all the coping patterns and beliefs that have stopped you facing your reality, and be truly honest with yourself about how any of these exercises apply to you.

UNDERSTANDING AND REMOVING YOUR INTER-FEAR-ANCES

Are there things that are stopping you from being who you want to be as a result of what we have learnt so far?

Are you letting your thoughts or feelings cloud your sense of reality? Have you climbed into a story or mental movie based on shoulds and shouldn'ts and are you allowing the events of your past to hold you back from your future?

119

How much of what you do is coming from the "Must be seen as ..." box, rather than from what is true for you and your needs, regardless of what society, your friends or your family think?

In addition to stories, ladder of inference, the drama triangle and guilt judgements, these are some of the other barriers I see mums having.

Looking back to the examples at the beginning of the book, let's examine what was happening for those mums.

I USED TO BE ABLE TO BUT I CAN'T DO THAT NOW!

Living on Comfort Zone Island

> *I heard myself as a full-time mum with both kids at school, saying to my husband: "Can't you phone the insurance company from the office about the quote, I just won't have time?"*

> *Three weeks back to work after maternity leave I am asked to head up a brand new project, I knew it was the chance I had been waiting for but was absolutely terrified... I realised that a day where I needed to pick up dry cleaning, a prescription, do the supermarket shopping and return library books around the school runs felt like an awfully busy day.*

> *Anything new, be it researching a new computer for my daughter or an energy provider for my house, had become a major task and was really rather frightening.*

As with all aspects of human interaction, a combination of different factors will be causing these kinds of feelings. My

own experience and that of the mums I know is that it can be attributed to some extent to two influences: a shrinking comfort zone, and straightforward fear.

Shrinking comfort zone
When we are catapulted into the world of motherhood, we suddenly discover what living outside of our comfort zone is all about. A baby states their feelings about the world the only way they can, with screams and cries, often very loudly and repeatedly. We need to work out how to feed, clothe, keep clean, comfort and stimulate this new child, discover how to set up car seats, buggies, prams, bath seats, baby gyms and every other piece of paraphernalia designed to test a *Krypton Factor* finalist, all while coming to terms with the effects of surgery or a battered pelvic floor and other complications, not to mention the 24-hour shifts, hormonal challenges and emotions that only seem to know the extreme settings of exhilaration and joy, often simultaneously with being overwhelmed and exhausted.

121

Then over time, by about three months, it seems that for most mums the world starts to re-form into a place that makes a kind of sense. (Believe me if you are still two months in, it does!)

Having our child continually with us, either physically or emotionally, we start to think ahead to meet their needs, in turn meeting ours – as a child whose needs are met is predominantly a contented child. Routines get set up, meeting friends with children, clubs, play dates, activities and fresh air options. The weeks start to revolve around our children and a level of stability can settle in. If life takes on an easier flow, a level of contentment can lead to a place of comfort. But if going back to work enters the equation, or any other major change – a house move, a subsequent pregnancy and many others – we are thrown straight back out of our comfort zone.

Don't get me wrong: being comfortable is a basic human need and a state to be embraced. However, psychology and many studies of the human mindset have shown repeatedly that a place of comfort has some potential pitfalls too. As we settle into any routine of having more events that we know and have handled many times before than challenging new events, our Comfort Zone Island unconsciously allows the range of things we do to deplete. Our world actually starts to shrink.

When a mum tells me she is "Happy just staying right where I am", that of course is fantastic; I am a little in awe and very respectful of mums who are always truly happy with their life. But I believe it is essential that we all understand one basic law of physics, the natural law that:

All things in the universe are either growing or decaying!

There is no standing still. By maintaining a way of living or believing that you are, you are in fact experiencing a form

122

of decaying. As with everything in nature, you can choose to grow or decay, whatever decaying may be for you. Once you're in a comfort zone, although at first it's a welcome relief, any attempts you make to escape that zone are tough, and by their very nature they cause discomfort.

A shrinking comfort zone happens quite slowly and insidiously, over months. Stress levels slowly increase about anything unknown or new and then one day coping with two children, having to make two admin phone calls, make a complaint at the local supermarket and setting up a new program for your child's homework suddenly becomes over-whelming. This can be a frightening place to be for someone who probably spent their pre-children life encountering new challenges and handling all manner of tasks.

Achievement expert Brian Tracy says, "90 to 95 percent of people will withdraw to the comfort zone when what they try doesn't work. Only that small percentage, 5 or 10 per-cent, will continually raise the bar on themselves; they will push themselves out into the zone of discomfort, and these are always the highest performers in every field."

So if in the past with a flash of insight you had decided to start a new campaign of achievement – a fitness regime, an evening class, studying or learning something new – the pain and discomfort may have overpowered you and sent you back to your comfort zone, now even more dissatisfied with yourself for having failed to meet the challenge.

Well, you and 95 per cent of the rest of the world too. Be kind to yourself and understand what happened. Know that through the journey you are taking with this book you are stacking the odds of success as high as you can and learning why you want to change. This time it will be different!

Leaving your comfort zone creates a temporary pain that every time beats the pain of atrophying further from the person you know you have the potential to be. Remember, we grow or we decay.

Cyclist Lance Armstrong put it this way:

Pain is temporary. It may last a minute, or an hour, or a day, or a year, but eventually it will subside and something else will take its place. If I quit however, it lasts forever.

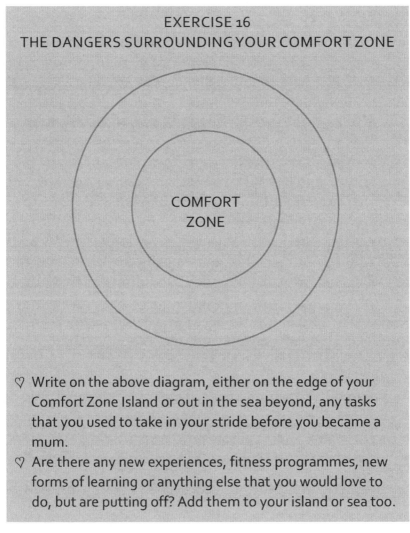

EXERCISE 16
THE DANGERS SURROUNDING YOUR COMFORT ZONE

COMFORT
ZONE

♡ Write on the above diagram, either on the edge of your Comfort Zone Island or out in the sea beyond, any tasks that you used to take in your stride before you became a mum.
♡ Are there any new experiences, fitness programmes, new forms of learning or anything else that you would love to do, but are putting off? Add them to your island or sea too.

♡ Then under the island, write the excuses you have unconsciously been developing – a poorly child, lack of sleep, a
play date, childcare issues, an abundance of housework,
visitors coming – to justify not doing these things.

How do you get off Comfort Zone Island?
There is an infinite base of evidence demonstrating the
indisputable rewards from stepping outside of your comfort
zone, stretching and improving yourself, growing and realising your potential. All it takes is a few small steps every
day.

For some mums, setting what feels like a terrifying,
seemingly unachievable goal motivates them:

♡ training as a teacher's assistant
♡ volunteering at a dogs' home
♡ taking a reiki course
♡ having a second child
♡ finding a new job
♡ learning to swim (at 41)
♡ setting up as a designer
♡ running 10k
♡ becoming a school governor
♡ writing a development book for mums

However, expanding your comfort zone does not have to
mean embarking on an Open University course, a new job
or any other huge, momentous event. The old adage applies:

*Do something new, something that feels slightly uncomfort-
able every day.*

Think about your values – moving outside your comfort zone
can be as simple as planning a new recipe for your family,
taking on new responsibilities at work, not getting involved
in the latest round of gossip, or joining the library and discovering a new author for both you and your children.

125

Find anything that expands who you currently are or currently know and then tell someone all about it and what you learnt from it. I will be helping you set personal goals at the end of the book. If you are stranded on Comfort Zone Island, make just one of your goals the one that will take you to a place where you are growing, not decaying.

Of course, for those of us who have gone back to work, who are currently surfing the wave of balancing both work and home challenges, the thought of a comfort zone is incredibly appealing. In fact, having just one day where life is not a rollercoaster would be wonderful. Yet neither extreme is useful or the best for your resourcefulness. You alone need to weigh up whether you are currently so far out of your comfort zone, or in practical terms giving so much to every commitment that you have taken on, that you will not be able to maintain the pace of life for much longer. An 18-hour day, where you are balancing the needs of your children, your team, your boss, your partner, your house and your family, is not sustainable long term without an acceptance that you need coping mechanisms. You have to take time to listen to your needs, not those as a career person or mum but you as a woman, the selfish not selfless one.

Being too far outside of your comfort zone is every bit as disabling as being stuck in a shrinking one. Remember this as you work through the rest of the book!

I'M JUST TOO SCARED!

Part of learning to understand and accept yourself is also realising what you can't do alone. For some of you, the emotional impact of becoming a mum may have had far deeper implications. Staying within a comfort zone for an extended period (I won't be specific as it is different for everyone) can actually lead to far stronger emotions than just discomfort. The feeling that can emerge is genuine fear.

Fear can be crippling, and I never underestimate the impact and power of being scared. As with other aspects of this book, A TRUTH will give you a mindset solution to overcoming and conquering your fear, but what I cannot gauge for you is how powerful and life altering your fears are to you. If you are currently aware that there are events, people or challenges that are causing you disabling, phobic levels of fear, if your fear is causing you to live in a way that is becoming unsustainable, my techniques will not bring you a solution. Ask yourself whether you need to seek more help.

As with all negative aspects affecting our mindset, everything from depression to anxiety and phobias, when we are experiencing them from within they can feel like a deep well of overwhelming confusion. The thought of the climb out feels far worse than sitting in the darkness, but believe me, the ropes available to climb up today are safe and strong.

Understanding the fear

We all have everyday fears, especially if we have done things in a similar way for a long time. If fear isn't a deep-set belief, nine times out of ten it is a particularly negative story. It is a story of:

False Evidence Appearing Real

Often an accumulation of feelings, needs and stories amalgamates into an insurmountable level of being overwhelmed.

In her book *Feel the Fear and Do It Anyway*®, Susan Jeffers examined fear and, utilising many tools including affirmations and thinking positive, she came up with many ideas about handling fear that remain relevant over 20 years later. She said that there are different types of fear, but for me, her bottom-line biggest fear, one that any mum sitting in a comfort zone can encounter, is the simple but all-powerful belief that you won't be able to handle something.

What do you think you wouldn't be able to handle?

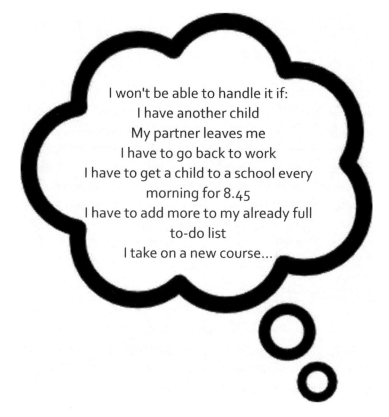

I won't be able to handle it if:
I have another child
My partner leaves me
I have to go back to work
I have to get a child to a school every
morning for 8.45
I have to add more to my already full
to-do list
I take on a new course...

To put it simply, Susan Jeffers advocates that the basic work to be done is to get to a point where you know you can handle anything that comes your way, bad and good. If you know you can handle anything that comes your way, the fear is greatly diminished. She approaches fear not as a psychological problem, but an educational one. She says that you must re-educate yourself to accept fear as a necessary part of growth, and then move yourself from the weakest to the strongest part of who you are. This is the same process we have already started with by working through A TRUTH. It is purely dissecting the story, unmet needs and feelings behind your fear and building a plan of action from the evidence base.

Jeffers sets out a number of "fear truths". For me the most relevant and profound is number five:

> *Pushing through fear is less frightening than living with the underlying fear that comes from a feeling of helplessness.*

In other words, those who never take any risks ironically live with a dread of something going wrong. They seek security above all else, but the effect is chronic insecurity. It is actually easier (and infinitely more life fulfilling) to try new things. The decision to incorporate more challenge into your life brings a feeling of security because you know you can tackle anything.

As her title says, "Feel the fear and do it anyway!"

For me this means feel the fear, acknowledge it to yourself, understand that you have it – then, using the tools that make you feel more powerful, dissect the story that it represents and move yourself forward.

Chloe had always dreamt of designing children's clothes. She had made a lot of her own children's clothes and she was always getting complimentary comments about what they wore.

She had mentioned her designing ambitions to her friends and husband and they all thought it was a great idea, but in three years of talking about it she had not moved any further forward. Her children were both now at school and she was getting more frustrated at herself for not doing anything about it.

When we talked, we analysed the worst-case scenarios of both starting the business and not starting.

Her worst fear about starting it was:

She might fail.

So we looked what failing would look like:

She would only invest the price of making the first few items and her time at four craft fairs in the summer.

Losing money is worth being afraid of, but what was the worst-case scenario? Failing would mean losing at worst £300 – was that worth the risk?

She would have invested her time and dreams and she would be broken-hearted if she failed.

One way of guaranteeing failure is never to try. Would she really feel worse if she had actually tried?

She didn't know where to start: business plans, networking, setting up a website etc.

When we analysed this, given the agencies available to new business people and the advice on the internet for entrepreneur mums, combined with the computer savvy of some of her friends, all of those fears were overcomable.

Seeing the best and the worst scenarios laid out in black and white, Chloe accepted that not doing it, and the years of fear thinking about it, were far worse than giving it a go.

So when facing your fear, find out the truth, if any, that it is based within.

The other piece of advice I endorse from Jeffers (I would definitely recommend her book if you are feeling overwhelmed by many fears) is to ask yourself:

What is the worst that can happen?

Look at the worst possible outcomes of facing your fear and their power over you will lessen. You will gain a different perspective.

Susan Jeffers works from a base of positive thinking. She recommends going for it and expecting the best, but letting go of the outcome, knowing that if it doesn't work out, you truly can handle it all. This is a powerful viewpoint which I agree with. Positive thinking helps us move forward, but in the beginning, some fears may need extra help to be overcome. I suggest that you explore the following.

Base your decision on reality, evidence and analysis:

- ♡ What negative outcomes could there be from facing the fear?
- ♡ What negative outcomes could there be from not facing the fear?

Then make a realistic, logical decision based on the balance of pros and cons of facing the fear.

EXERCISE 17
ANALYSE YOUR FEAR

Look at the list of situations, activities and tasks in the last exercise that you are overwhelmed by and putting off. Choose the most important to you, the one you really wish you could overcome.

♡ Analyse the facts this fear is based on. (Remember: Is that true?)

♡ Ask yourself: What is the worst that can happen from facing this fear?

♡ Ask yourself: What is the worst that can happen by not facing this fear? (Think again of what your children are saying about your life at your funeral.)

♡ Which outcome sits within your personal values?

Weigh up these lists and assess whether you, with your new-found self-awareness and building confidence, should face your fear and do it anyway, or get help to face your fear and do it anyway?

UNDERSTANDING WHAT YOU CAN ACTUALLY CHANGE

One final element I feel is relevant is one that I have been utilising for myself and my clients for many years.

Only work within the realities of what is possible, what you can change.

This is a very simple way to gain understanding and acceptance when you feel powerless and overwhelmed. Examine what you can do instead of focusing on worries over which you have no real control. First, become more aware of all of your worries:

My worries:
Health   Child development   Career development
Finances   Relationship   Sanity   Success

Then analyse those worries and determine where you can take action, those which you actually have some control over or where you can influence the outcome:

> My worries that can be influenced:
> My thoughts and actions
> Organisation and time management
> Saying no to less important things

Only focus your time and energy on those which you have some influence over. Think of ways to be more proactive and address the things you can do something about. This will lessen the amount of time you spend worrying about things that you can do nothing about. In time the worries that you can't control will lessen and your ability to feel in control of your life will grow.

Let me demonstrate.

Philippa's daughter had chronic eczema. She had researched every avenue of help that she could, both conventional and alternative. She acknowledged that her levels of worry and stress around her daughter's eczema were suspending her in a place where she couldn't move forward, and that fear was holding her back.

She worried about chemicals in other people's houses, play groups and parks and so kept her daughter predominantly at home. She worried about what other mums and children might say to her daughter, knocking what she already believed to be a shaky level of self-esteem. She spent a great deal of time worrying about the weather, as hot temperatures made her daughter substantially worse. She felt she was being organised and proactive about the condition, but she also knew she had lost both perspective and control over its effects on both her daughter and her.

When listing all of her worries, it soon became clear that there were some, such as the weather, that although she could plan and prepare for, she could gain nothing from getting stressed about. She had absolutely no control over what the weather would be like. She could not influence what chemicals others used in their environments, but she could ask, and act appropriately depending on the level of effect they would have.

Philippa worked through all her worries and fears, found the evidence base within them all and then concentrated only on the ones she had influence over. Her daughter's life is still filled with challenges, but Philippa faces them with a stronger sense of perspective and feeling calmer than she did before.

BUT WHAT IF...?

Something very unexpected happened for me when I became a mum. Along with the depth of love and protection

I felt for my children came a level of almost incomprehensible fear. From the day you carry that tiny baby out to the car for the first time and drive home slower than a geriatric milk float, you suddenly embrace the fear of something terrible happening to this innocent creature that you love more than life itself. The love is overwhelming, but with that comes the mini movies you create of their imminent danger.

When walking downstairs holding them tight, an instant image flashes into your mind of you slipping, dropping the baby and him or her falling. You walk past hot cookers and see saucepan handles hanging over and sharp knives on surfaces that just might jump off and attack your charge, who isn't even crawling let alone able to pull down a knife. Cot death, swine flu, car accidents, drowning, poisoning, asphyxiation, earthquakes, tidal waves and alien abduction... all suddenly become acutely real and possible.

There are real risks to our children, and for some unfortunately the worst can and does happen. Learning to cope, rebuild and carry on after a tragedy is a journey some mothers have to travel, and that is reality and heartbreakingly sad.

The fact is, however – and you know me by now, I like to work with the facts – it is not the norm. For the majority of mums, the worst will *not* happen to their children. What I do believe can be a potential hazard to them is learning inappropriate fear.

We should prepare our children for the real dangers of the world, for example teaching them how to be aware of hazards, hot surfaces, plugs, crossing the road, strangers. However, when I ask mums to list the characteristics they hope for their children when they grow up, courage is often high on the list, nearly always in the top ten.

The fear of losing a child and the strength of wanting to protect your children is natural, instinctive and primeval.

It is Mother Nature's way of equipping you with the strengths you need to protect and nurture the next generation. What is not resourceful is when your fears for them start to inappropriately inhibit their instinctive courage.

Only you will know if you are operating in the realm of overprotection and being overly cautious with your children. What I would ask of you is to keep checking in with yourself on what you are showing your children about courage. The movies of flying knives, demon kidnappers or killer bees may still play in your mind, but what is crucial is that you rationalise their impact by not letting them flow into the tip of your iceberg with your actions and words. Remember that your children are always watching you, they learn their boundaries of the world from your behaviours.

Also if the movies do get too much, *don't* scan the internet for statistics and jump at the first search result. It is our natural instinct to protect our children and we all have some level of fear about their development or safety. *Don't* panic until you have a fully rounded picture of all the facts about your fear and start to build some perspective. *Do* talk to those around you, share your fear and start to gain perspective and balance about what you are worried about.

UNDERSTANDING THE IMPORTANCE OF HAPPINESS

Of course, my wish for us all is ultimately happiness, but I believe that the best reality is a balance of experiencing more happiness than sadness, as through our life there will be both and lots of time spent somewhere in between. Expecting the best and preparing for the worst allows us to be OK with whichever shows up.

You are the only person responsible for your happiness. I don't need to understand what will make you happy, but you do. This chapter will bring some general quick fixes based on a mass of evidence to build a positive frame of mind, and will take you on a journey to establish what the long-term solutions are for you to take responsibility for your happiness.

First and foremost, there is one element of positive thinking for which the evidence base is unequivocal, the positive effects of being happy. Happiness not only makes us feel better, it actually brings greater levels of success in both our personal and professional life.

> *Finding happiness is like finding yourself. You don't find happiness, you make happiness. You choose happiness. Self-actualization is a process of discovering who you are, who you want to be and paving the way to happiness by doing what brings YOU the most meaning and content-ment to your life over the long run.*
> **—David Leonhardt, The Happy Guy**

Happiness is something I hope for every day and I find a way to end a day happy with what it brought. As paradoxical as it sounds, I choose to be happy about being sad, scared, lonely, bitter, angry, whatever shows up, as happiness for me is acceptance of my reality, not fighting it.

Make a start by purely thinking happy thoughts, laughing at a joke or a funny cartoon. In this way you actually create happy hormones and chemicals. The happy chemical signals stay in your body and allow you to radiate happiness into your subsequent behaviour and interactions long after you stop laughing.

The best prescription for happiness is to make a point of finding people, situations and books that make you smile and repeat that as many times a day as you can. It may sound trite and simplistic, but it works!

WAKE UP AND SMELL THE FRESH BREAD

Another way of provoking happiness is to refresh your memory frequently about the things you have that you are incredibly grateful for.

Professor Richard Wiseman explains that when you walk into a room that smells of freshly baked bread, you quickly detect the gorgeous aroma. However, stay in the room for a few minutes and the smell will disappear. The only way to re-awaken it is to walk out of the room and back in again.

Exactly the same concept applies to happiness and appreciation. We all have something amazing to be appreciative of.

However, as time passes we get used to what we have, and these wonderful assets disappear from our minds. By reminding ourselves of what we have to be grateful for, in essence we keep re-entering the room with the enticing smell of fresh bread and the warmth that brings.

The two other acts that are proven to bring happiness are, first, not spending money on possessions – psychology maintains that retail therapy, just like a strong coffee, brings a temporary high and then a mood slump – but buying things for others. The act of giving creates happiness and it doesn't have to be a money-based gift: the gift of time, emotions (a hug) or just listening not only gives something to the recipient but also gives you a sense of happiness.

The second is creating experiences for yourself, with your children, your friends and your partner, where you can share joy and wonder, again creating all the happy chemicals you need.

That's a wonderful excuse to leave work early or forget the housework, the laundry and the to-do list and run off with your kids to the nearest park or your back garden and play, run, bounce, skip and laugh. I can guarantee that your children and you will remember the times you let the chores go and played instead. They will catch happiness from you and I can't imagine wishing anything more for my boys than knowing how to embrace happiness.

EXERCISE 18
WHAT ARE YOU GRATEFUL FOR?

Write down all the things in your life that you are grateful for, everything from your children, your career, to the two-minute rest with a cup of coffee that you managed to have today. (Repeat this exercise every time you find yourself feeling sad or frustrated with your life.)

Find something – a favourite book, an old episode of *Friends*, a friend you know will make you laugh, a game of tickling with your children – and let yourself smile, laugh, giggle and embrace happiness. It is good for your health!

Go on, I know you have it in you somewhere!

I CAN'T CHANGE THE REST OF THE WORLD!

So far on our journey to find A TRUTH, we have explored the inter-fear-ances you may be experiencing and becoming aware of your thoughts, feelings and needs. Your journey within is now underway, and we are now going to start looking at the world around you and understanding how you fit into it. You will have begun to feel more satisfied and at peace with the mum you are – now I am going to show you areas where you can start to change, influence or accept, as reality permits, the world around you.

When you were a child, you believed that anything could be yours. The world was an amazing place, full of dreams and expectations that were all there for you. You may see this now in your children. Remember their journey of learning to walk (or if they haven't got that far or it was not possible, making any significant physical advance). Recall the collection of knocks, scrapes, bumps and bruises. Remember the unbridled bravery, courage, excitement and determination despite the greatest of knockbacks.

You too had that bravery, determination, excitement and courage once, and you still do. The potential to feel all of these things does not die, it is a synaptic pathway in our brain that was created and remains in the depths of our human potential.

Over time, the reality of our lives influences our thoughts and beliefs. We find there are some things that pure determination and effort can't win; we don't achieve everything we set out to do. We fill our lives with obligations, other people's needs, responsibilities, mortgages, loans, partners to find compatible compromises with, children to love, feed and clothe. Along the way our perspective changes.

140

EXERCISE 19
WHERE IS YOUR INNER CHILD?

What did you want to be when you were 3, 5 and 10? (Can you remember that far back?)

Did you have any strong beliefs that you fought for through your teenage years (either with your parents, your friends, school or society)?

When did you last feel truly passionate about something and follow that passion through with determination and make something happen? (Have you ever?)

For this next step I would ask you to think back to how much belief, passion and determination it must have taken for you to learn to walk, or to achieve all the things you have so far in your life, and face these next sections with the excitement you saw or see in your children.

WHERE ARE YOU?

We covered in the story section that many of your thoughts and feelings may arise from stories where you argue with the reality of the situation. Once you have reached the truth of the situation, discovered your needs and assessed your subsequent feelings, you may have more resourceful feelings, but you're still standing in the same place. You need to establish a starting point for the world around you, a reality check, a stocktake on where you are operating from.

Any of you who have undertaken any coaching pro-gramme, life coaching or personal development will have encountered this first exercise before, some of you many times. I make no apology for asking you to complete it again.

For me it still, after all its years in circulation, gives us a clear, graphical demonstration of where any imbalances may sit in our lives. Answer it for today, for this week, for this month, look clearly and concisely at how your overall life looks to you right now. For those of you who have not com-pleted it before, I am including comprehensive instructions.

EXERCISE 20
YOUR WHEEL OF LIFE

(More wheels available on the website www.theonlymum.com.)

Consider all the topics on the wheel of life shown opposite, and work around the wheel addressing each one in turn. Sup-posing that 10 (the outer edge of the circle) is "Couldn't be bet-ter" and 0 (the circle's centre) is "Couldn't be worse", score yourself in terms of contentment in each area by marking the lines of the wheel with a dot of one colour, paying attention only to how things are for you right now. Then join the dots, as shown in the example at the top.

This example shows that I'm just starting an exercise routine, but I only manage it two days a week, so my Health and Fitness score currently feels like a 2 to me. However, I've just moved near to the sea and decorated my house, so my Physical Environment is a 9.

UNDERSTANDING WHO YOU ARE

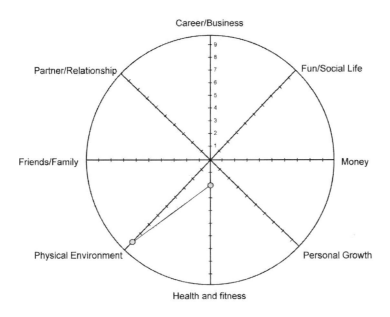

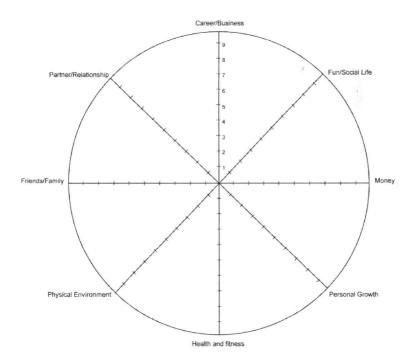

Now ask yourself how much importance you place on each of these life areas, with 0 being "Low priority" and 10 being "High priority". For example, if having fun is really important to you and money is less so, you might score these as 9 and 2 respectively – a recognition of the fact that money is useful but not of great value to you. Mark these scores and join the dots in the same way as before, but in a different colour.

Finally, think back over a typical recent fortnight in your life. Mark on the circle in a third colour how much time you'd normally spend on each area, then join these dots. In this instance, 0 is "A little", 10 is "A lot".

♡ What do you notice from your wheel?

♡ What is it saying to you?

♡ Do you have a balanced wheel?

♡ Are you focusing your time and effort on the areas that mean the most to you?

♡ Do you feel anything that you didn't expect or that surprises you?

♡ Do you recognise certain things that were bound to show up and you are already aware of?

This is a very clear demonstration of how you see your life balance currently. It gives you a starting point for working out what your gaps are, where imbalances exist between your values and your hopes, and the reality of the way you are living now. Keep your wheel to hand, as it is the first step towards building your future goals. We will be using this and what you have learnt in the future goal setting we do later in the book.

UNDERSTANDING THOSE WHO MATTER MOST

By definition as mums we do not exist in isolation. You also need to establish where the people around you fit in to your future goals.

Experts say that becoming parents together is the point at which nearly half of marriages flounder. According to a 2003 review of 90 studies, only 38 per cent of women with babies are likely to report being very happy in their marriage, compared with 62 per cent of childless women. (Not great, is it?) In 2004, the National Marriage Project at Rutgers University went so far as to proclaim that "children seem to be a growing impediment for the happiness of marriages". However, research also shows that children raised by happy couples are more likely to grow up to have their own healthy relationships. That is the reality from the statistics, but how is that useful?

You started this book looking at the idealised image that you consciously or unconsciously measure yourself against as a mum. This expectation of yourself and the state of motherhood has been formed over your lifetime, more often than not from your own childhood and your own mum. Through the course of this book you are re-examining those expectations of yourself and resetting your vision of motherhood. What you also have to be aware of is the unwritten, unspoken expectations you have of all the other people around you: what the father of your child should be like, how your own parents and parents-in-law should be. And what qualities and attributes should friends and colleagues bring to parenthood?

It's that word **should** again! You build your expectations on a cocktail of societal influence, the media, your own socialisation and childhood, and the prejudices and stories that come from a lifetime of growing into parenthood. Right now you are judging, holding feelings about and living with those around you carrying these expectations and your perceived feelings about how each individual is measuring up for you. And they are doing the same for you.

About six months into the life of our first child, my husband and I had the biggest argument of our lives together to that point. It was an explosion of unmet needs, unheard feelings, deep-set resentment and, of course, our exhaustion as a consequence of having and loving a baby who didn't sleep. It was a ferocious, hurtful, explosive, over-the-top outburst of massive pain.

When the initial explosion had passed and we were slowly and tentatively working through the fall-out (we both teach this stuff, can you imagine the communication in our house?), one thing became very clear to us both. More than anything we were disappointed and frustrated in the way the other person was behaving, based on a comparison to a belief or expectation about how we thought they should have been that, first, we didn't even realise we had and, secondly, we had never shared with each other.

Start by working through your most important relationships and examining how strong you feel they currently are.

EXERCISE 21
WHO DO YOU LOVE?

Stop and think about the following.

From your heart, and from your whole life, list the friends, family members, colleagues or professionals that you, either historically or currently, trust with your dreams, your fears, your joy and your pain. These are the people you cannot imagine losing from your life.

Now look at the list and note next to each name the last time you saw them. (Not on Facebook, Friends Reunited or any other social media group, Skype or email, but when you last actually saw, touched or held them.)

Thirdly, note the last time you complimented, thanked or showed some appreciation to that person for being in your life.

If there are people on this list for which you wish you could answer these questions differently, make your first step on this external journey to be changing any sadness or regret by taking the relevant action.

The people around you have the potential to create challenges for you, but they are also the foundations of your mental health and happiness. Having a support network of people whom you love and who love you is essential for living with joy and confidence. We all need someone to share, confide, laugh and cry with. They are a vehicle for releasing all our feelings, needs and stories and relieving the pressure cooker of emotions within.

YOUR OWN MUM

I am lucky enough that for the early years of my boys' lives, my mum is alive, fit and well. We live close to her and she is able to see us every week, something my children really love and look forward to. At times she has been not only my mum when I have felt like a child, but my plumber, electrician, nurse, chef, gardener, bedtime supervisor and emergency babysitter.

When I became a mum, my feelings about my mum changed; I had entered the arena I had grown up watching her navigate. I know how lucky I am to be able to gain that awareness while I can still share it with my mum.

It is different becoming a mum when you never knew or no longer have your mum, if she is far away, she is unwell, or your relationship has broken down. Maybe you already are or are on the threshold of becoming your mum's carer. All these situations can potentially be another area where pain or unhappiness, or inter-fear-ance, may occur for you.

Psychology has always placed a great deal of responsibility on our maternal relationships and that still holds true. Many believe that who we are as people is to a large part honed by what we saw in our mum. The same is true for our own children (what a responsibility!). Your experience of being a mum will have come predominantly from the woman who mothered you. It may be a key emotional factor in how you view yourself as a mum and deserves some thought and reflection.

EXERCISE 22
HOW DO YOU THINK ABOUT YOUR MUM?

Take time, be kind to yourself and acknowledge how becoming a mum has altered your feelings about your own mum, either positively or negatively.

You will also have had expectations about the role your mum would or would not play in your children's lives. If she is not here for you, is that in any sense causing you emotions that are worth acknowledging?

You potentially will have had similar hopes of your father and other relatives, and how they are performing against those hopes will be causing you to have feelings and display behaviours to those around you.

Take time to examine how you feel about your closest family members and how they contribute to your life and you to theirs since becoming a mum.
　　Are they doing what you hoped they would?

BUT THINGS HAVE CHANGED SINCE I WAS A CHILD!

My husband and I in our own inimitable way at first superseded any words of experience from our mums in favour of our new book-learnt skills, friends' experiences and the development we had undergone throughout our lives. We did fully believe that things had changed since our mums had brought us up. We unconsciously had formed judgements from the memories of our childhoods of what we would not do. Only as time passed did we realise that the patterns we observed and took on by osmosis as children from our parents are still with us. We need to remain aware that we only allow the ones we would choose to show up in the way we parent our boys. We also gained an insight into the women our mums became and changed our view of them from those observations.

EXERCISE 23
ARE YOU THE SAME AS YOUR MUM?

Think back to your childhood and without judgement answer the following:

What behaviours did you see in your mum that you hope you emulate?

What behaviours did you see in your mum that you hope you don't emulate?

Did your mum work or was she at home full time?

Do you?

While psychology tells us that we unconsciously take our learned behaviours from what we observed as children, neuroscience and advances in psychology show us that although we can't unlearn these memories, these mental pathways of experience, we can choose not to act on them.

Emi had grown up in a happy family, one where both parents held both cultural respect and manners in very high regard. Emi had learnt to stem some of her more exuberant personality traits to conform to the girl her mum in particular wanted her to be.

In her twenties she had developed awareness that the constraints she had grown up with were no longer useful for her and the person she wanted to be. She married outside of her culture and her relationship with her mum really suffered.

When Emi became a mum, she attempted to rebuild her relationship with her mum, trying to involve her in her grandchildren's lives. She had set clear boundaries with her mother that the children were to be allowed to grow up differently than she had and her mum was keeping her opinions to herself. However, on a number of occasions she had found herself angry with or embarrassed by her children's completely natural tendency to ignore or rebel against manners and etiquette.

She had started to place importance on the very things she had rebelled against in her life, things that she really didn't want to punish or shame her children with, and yet she was.

As Emi began to understand that she absorbed many unconscious values from her parents, she was more able to accept and then choose different responses to them.

If you know that you have an outstanding conversation, a setting of boundaries, a show of appreciation, forgiveness or acceptance to share with your mum, or her memory, find the time to do so.

TO WORK OR NOT TO WORK?

Well, that really is the question. I joked at the beginning of the book about the myths we hear about in the media and the impressions others get about both working and full-time mums. About 60 per cent of mums now go back to work before their children start school; in our mothers' day the percentage was far lower, in fact about half that of today. Many of us and our partners grew up believing that mum was at home for us, and that will have created expectations, feelings and potential areas of inadequacy within us.

Society and the media bombard us with a confusing plethora of role-model working mums and full-time mums surrounded with domestic bliss. The messages are confusing and potentially unsettling. In the process of my research for this book and the mums I have worked with I have seen and heard myriad stories, worries, justifications and emotions from both working and full-time mums about the expectations that society, their families, their employers and they themselves place on them about going back to work.

I have chosen to go back to work. I was a frustrated and unfulfilled full-time mum and my mental realisation that I would be a better mum if I worked was one I resisted at first, worrying about the effect on my boys and what others would think. I know I was very lucky to have the choice: many of you will have gone back to work as a necessity, to keep your families financially afloat or quite simply because there is only you who could be the financial provider.

Some of you could be at home full time, feeling on the one hand that you are doing the right thing for your children, but confused as a part of you feels unfulfilled and worried that you are atrophying as a person. For some of you being at home with your children may be the happiest and most fulfilled you have ever been. Many of you, like me, will

152

always have planned to go back to work and when the time came either found bridging the gap between motherhood and career challenging, or simply felt either exhausted with the physical hours worked or the mental worry of the consequences of your choice.

What is crucial is that you examine mentally what being a working or full-time mum means to you and whether you are emotionally at peace with the situation you are in.

Check in with yourself when you meet or have in the past met a truly happy full-time or working mum, how you feel about that mum. What inner dialogue are you hearing? It will give you some clues as to how you are feeling and talking to yourself.

EXERCISE 24
AM I DOING WHAT I WANT TO DO?

♡ In an ideal world, no financial implications, no guilt at the possible effects on your children, would you choose to be at work or be a full-time mum?

♡ Is that your true answer or what you think society, your employer, your partner or your friends think you should be doing?

♡ If you are not able to live your choice, what is stopping you?

♡ How do you feel about the barriers, people or needs that stop you from living as you would choose? (List all your emotions, hear and acknowledge them, allow them to be real.)

♡ Can you influence or change any of those barriers in any other way?

♡ If the reality is that you cannot live your ideal choice, how will you choose to live with that? Will you accept and make the best of it, or will you carry resentment and pain?

(Look again at the Understanding the fear section and work through any strong feelings that you may be experiencing.)

Resentment is like drinking poison and waiting for the other person to die. —**Carrie Fisher**

MUM FRIENDS

When we became mums, many of us will have searched out a circle of support from fellow mums in the same place as us, traversing the same challenges and encountering the same obstacles and joys. These mum friends can be the backbone for releasing our fears, our concerns, our pride and our achievements. Today we have social networking sites, rekindling old friend sites and a massive resource of a group of friendly ears. Use your extended network, give to it and be active in searching out and returning support.

The evidence base shows that not only is friendship key to our happiness and indeed our health, the need for community with other women is biological; it is part of our DNA. *The Tending Instinct* by Shelley E. Taylor consolidates a variety of studies covering cultural factors, decades of research, anecdotal references – even the biological ties to the girlfriend concept in the animal kingdom. It helps define why we as women are more social, more community focused, collaborative and less competitive and, above all, why we need our girlfriends.

It concludes that women with strong female ties (girl-friends) and female family have a longer life expectancy than those without them. In fact, women without strong social ties have the relative health risks equivalent to being overweight or a smoker. Both because of the oxytocin released when we are with good female friends and the emotional benefits of sharing worries and troubles with them, friendships can actually release stress and make us live longer.

That's a legitimate excuse for a girls' night out!

If you do only one thing as a result of reading this book, make it that you reignite or seek out female friendships that have the potential to bring you and allow you to give love and laughter and to share improved health and vitality.

A RELATIONSHIP AUDIT

As well as your loved ones and your friends, day to day your thriving and surviving as a mum requires the input of others. These people may not be your best friends but teachers, bosses, colleagues, childcare workers, swimming teachers, coaches and many others. Your relationship and communication with them are as essential as they would be in a workplace, as together they have an input on you and probably your children's experience of life.

In your life now, list the five adults you interact with the most day to day, be they friends, family, your partner, or anyone else. These are the people who make up your current support network:

We are going to go through a two-stage process, examining your relationship with each of these people.

155

EXERCISE 25
HOW WELL ARE YOU GETTING ON?

On pages 158–62, you'll see a calibration scale like the one below. There's one for each of the five people you listed. Without rationalising or analysing for too long, ask yourself what you think your level of communication and mutual support is with each person. Plot it on the scale as a tick, a cross, or a smiley or sad face – it's up to you. (Again, you can find more calibration scales on my website, www.theonlymum.com.)

Total failure   **High level**

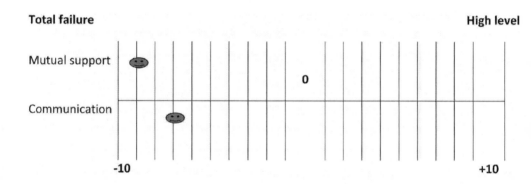

Mutual support

0

Communication

-10   +10

This exercise is completely subjective, so don't try to be logical or rational about it. Ask yourself what the answers are and see what comes back. Judge your relationship with each person right now. Then go back and for each person answer the two questions underneath the scale.

My own answers relating to the scale above are given opposite.

My friend Claudia

Why have I scored myself as I have with this person?

♡ I see my friend Claudia nearly every day. I feel that our relationship has become functional, based on the stresses and
routine of being mums. I have stopped feeling that I support
her as we are both too caught up in our day-to-day tasks. All I
seem to do is moan to her these days, which does fulfil one
need in me, but falls short of what I would hope to bring to
our relationship. I don't feel that we are growing together and
bringing out the best in each other any more. I can't remember the last time we laughed or had a happy story to share
and I would like to change that.

What actions can I take so that I can score myself more positively
with this person (if applicable)?

♡ I sat down with Claudia, apologised for being so caught up in
my world and we worked out how we can get more fun into
our friendship again. (Suffice to say, chocolate and wine
played a large part in our plan!)

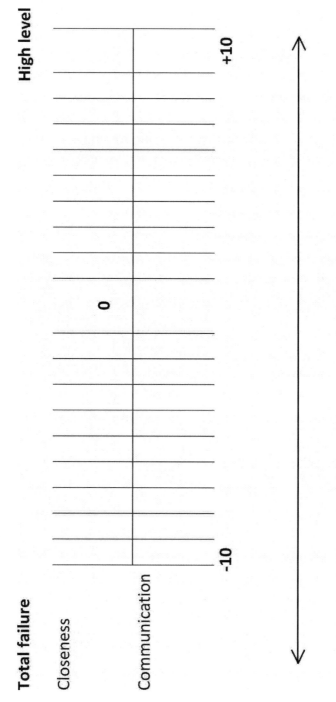

Total failure   High level

Closeness

Communication

-10   0   +10

1. Why have I scored myself as I have with this person?

2. What actions can I take so that I can score myself more positively with this person (if applicable)?

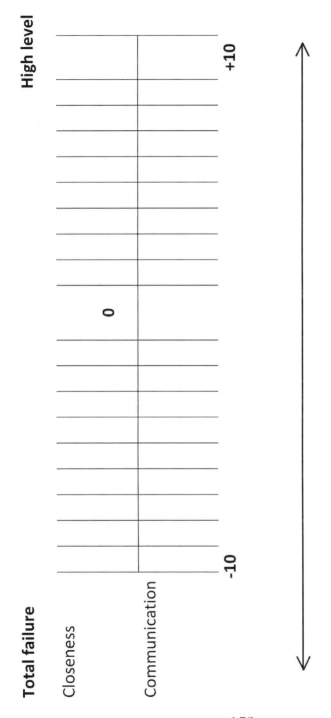

1. Why have I scored myself as I have with this person?

2. What actions can I take so that I can score myself more positively with this person (if applicable)?

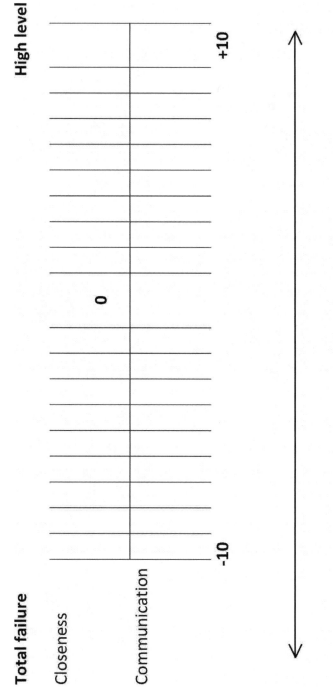

High level

Total failure

Closeness

Communication

+10

0

-10

1. Why have I scored myself as I have with this person?

2. What actions can I take so that I can score myself more positively with this person (if applicable)?

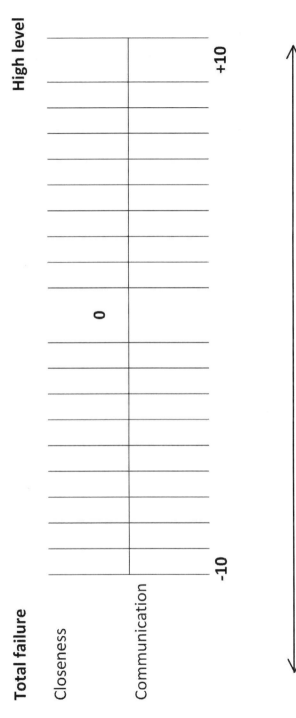

Total failure

Closeness

Communication

High level

+10

0

-10

1. Why have I scored myself as I have with this person?

2. What actions can I take so that I can score myself more positively with this person (if applicable)?

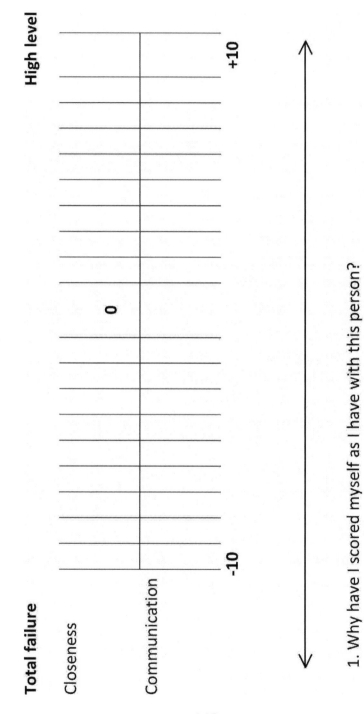

Total failure

Closeness

Communication

High level

0

+10

-10

1. Why have I scored myself as I have with this person?

2. What actions can I take so that I can score myself more positively with this person (if applicable)?

The five people you interact with as a mum every day are essential to you being the mum you want to be. Equally, you also have the responsibility to ensure that you are supporting, encouraging, sharing with and looking after them and your relationship with them.

We often seek out in others either what we want for ourselves or see lacking in ourselves. Look at the people you love, the people you spend your time with, and know that at some unconscious level, as cold as it sounds, they are meeting a need for you. Of course you are meeting a need for them too. That is friendship, in its essence, or how it should be. One sometimes painful step of self-awareness and loving the people around us is working out when we have chosen people who reinforce parts of us which we are not aware of and may not want to keep. Think about whether any of that is true for you.

EXERCISE 26
MAKE THE CHANGES WITH THE PEOPLE WHO MATTER MOST, NOW!

Look at the actions you believe you can take and start to put more small steps of encouragement, appreciation and awareness into each relationship.

Choose how you can further enhance the lives of those who influence and support you and your children.

ARE YOU A PLOM AT A PITY PARTY?

Both as a mum and as a human being, it is very easy to fall into poor little old meing, or PLOMing.

Have you ever sat with your friends and started to have a bit of a rant about, say, your partner? It starts with "You won't believe what he said last night..." and ends with your friends proclaiming "Oh my God, I can't believe he said that, he is unbelievable!"

How often do your friends disagree and rationalise with you? Do they say "Don't be so hard on him, he is loving, tolerant, a great dad, and successful too"? How much more likely is it that they join in? "Oh my God! My husband is even worse, he can't even..."

We often surround ourselves with people we can air our frustrations with. It's a part of friendship that is cathartic and useful, but one downside is they can not only reinforce our negative thoughts about other people, but enhance them and make them seem real.

We now know that most of these rants are based on stories, but others saying the same about the characters in our stories just allows us to add more evidence and build the potentially negative associated feelings for that person.

What starts out as a friendly get-together often turns into an unplanned pity party.

A FUN EXERCISE
OVERHEARING A PITY PARTY

Imagine that you have two hours all to yourself, no work, no chores to do, no kids, no social commitments (I know, it sounds unbelievable... but give it a go!). You choose to go and sit in your local coffee shop, have a very large piece of chocolate fudge cake with your latte and read a completely vacuous gossip magazine. As you settle down, you become aware that next to you is a group of new mums, who are in deep conversation in a truly cathartic pity party.

As you overhear them, imagine the things in their life that they could be moaning about. Write them on the mums' moan list below. There are some examples overleaf.

Mums' moan list

OTHER MUMS' MOAN LIST

I'm so tired
I do exist... I am more than just your mum...
I just want 5 minutes' peace, 5 minutes for me!
He/she just won't sleep/eat/crawl/walk...
He/she just doesn't listen
He/she just doesn't think
Oh my God... another meal to prepare!
More washing?!
No! Not another bug...
No! Not another smelly nappy...
Sex, what does he mean we don't have enough sex?
Sorry, I'm late... again
"Get your shoes on, now!!"
"Pick up those towels/coats/shoes/toys... now"
"Just a few more mouthfuls..."
"School note, what school note?"
"I don't care if EVERYONE else has one..."
"You are right! I don't understand you"
"How can the fridge be empty and the washing basket full, already?"

Does every mum feel like this?

Well, surprise! We are all feeling the same sometimes, and we can share and sympathise with all of those feelings.

Where self-awareness comes is in the ability to acknowledge the negatives but balance them with the reality and the positives that it brings.

A pity party just reinforces all our negative stories about the people we love and surround ourselves with. The danger is, as we know, that we can behave towards and treat people according to the stories we have created for them. When those stories are fired up and reinforced by others, it is easy to jump up our ladder of inference and communicate with the rest of the world purely filled with unresourceful feelings.

The other challenge with pity parties is that they often focus on things we have no influence over. So we get stuck in our circle of concern and can start to feel helpless again.

When we continuously tell ourselves that life is tough and we can do nothing about it, we fall into a place called learned helplessness, and we keep shrinking our comfort zone as we become overcome with fear that we are unable to influence anything. This is a path far from the journey that you have begun with this book, and having travelled it a few times in my life I would not recommend it.

You now know there is a second path, but it may mean making a few social changes for a while. Only you know what those are.

If you can remain aware of what is happening and gain pleasure and support from attending pity parties (I still do), then please share them with your friends and rant to your heart's content. However, if part of your values and your hopes for the mum you want to be focuses on the balanced reality and the part you play in others' behaviour towards you, you may want to avoid getting caught up in the story of what they don't do.

If you are too new along the path of awareness to be able to remain strong when all around you are PLOMing, you may have to step back from pity parties for a while, or share what you are learning with your friends and start getting and giving reinforcement for the strengths of those around you.

It's your call!

WHAT DID YOU EXPECT?

One of the biggest areas of discontentment in the relationships surrounding a mum is the ways people perform against the unwritten, undiscussed, often unknown expectations of each other. Your partner, mother, friends and family all had an image, an expectation of how you would act as a mum. They may not be aware of it yet, but they are also measuring your performance against a standard they laid down unconsciously in their childhood. How you perform against that image and expectation will be forming unconscious stories for them as well. These feelings will be contributing to their behaviours and actions towards you that may influence how you grow as a mum. You therefore need to complete your picture of the reality of where you are now with them, before you can move forward to find out what the future will look like.

In a work setting you would not expect to plunge into a new project with no idea of which member of the project team is doing what and what their expectations, roles and responsibilities are. Yet for the biggest, lifetime project of them all, becoming parents, we often dive in with no discussion of future roles and expectations, and little discussion of what shared success or perceived failure would look like.

I'm not sure it is realistic or practical for couples and their support network to work out in-depth roles until people actually start to live through parenthood. However, for those of us who are deep into our parenting role, there has to be a point where the time spent on these discussions circumvents the time spent feeling resentful, distressed or unhappy at where people are not meeting your expectations and you theirs. So is now the time for you?

Studies show that women who work outside of the home tend to do about three times more domestically than men after a child is born – yet I guarantee your partner will feel like he got the short end of the stick and will claim that he contributes at a percentage far higher than you do. Why? Relationship therapist Sabitha Pillai-Friedman points out, "Even though a lot of men say, 'I want to do 50 percent of everything', if they grew up in a traditional family, it's very hard for them to break that mould."

So while your partner congratulates himself on changing more nappies than his own father did, you're angry because you're still handling three out of four. I can't tell you what the correct balance is, but I do think that the two of you can, and starting to discuss it or working it out between you is a good first step.

I am including two expectations exercises in this interlude. The first is an in-depth needs- and feelings-based discussion with a long introduction and explanation. It could take an hour, it could take days or even the rest of your relationship to complete. (Seriously, it could!)

The second is a fun, top-line, task-based expectations evaluation, which requires far less emotional input and will allow you and the closest people to you to share a common understanding of your day-to-day task expectations. Choose which will work best for you and your life.

OPTIONAL EXERCISE: NEEDS-BASED EXPECTATION AUDIT

I do know that of all the exercises in this book, this will be one of the most challenging. First, it involves discussing with those closest to you both their and your perceptions of each other. This will mean potentially hearing feedback and observations that don't fit with your own and all the emotional challenges associated with that.

I do recommend that you undertake this exercise with the two essential people in your life. However, I have been on the receiving end of my husband and friends coming back from courses or finishing reading a book and bombarding me with a quiz or an exercise, claiming to know what I am doing wrong or how I should be acting or feeling. Nothing is more annoying, even if their intention is completely pure.

My advice would be to read through the exercise first by yourself. Be realistic: will these discussions bring you anything positive, or could they present more challenges? Are you mentally ready, willing and able to be aware and responsible through the discussions? Remember, the person you are talking with has not read this book and will not have been on the self-awareness journey that you have. Decide if there is anything to be gained by getting them to work through it too and then find the words to share with them why and what you would like to do with them.

Is this really going to add to your relationship?
I am a qualified mediator, I have seen how simple discussions where the stakes are at their highest, giving personal feedback to those you love, can quickly move from an adult-to-adult, rational discussion to a distressing child-like argument, coming from hurt pride and feelings. So this section

170

comes with a health warning. I am not a qualified relation-ship counsellor, I am giving you material that I use with executives and mums in my seminars that is written by psy-chologists and life coaches. The ideal situation would be for me to be on hand to work through the exercise with you, but that obviously is not possible.

Our key relationships can be the backbone of our exis-tence, both as a mum and as a woman, and as such they are also the biggest threat to our mental health and stability if they are dysfunctional. I would definitely not recommend entering into the following discussions if you believe they could lead to distress or discomfort that is beyond a level that your self-awareness alone can cope with.

As you complete this exercise, mentally check whether you are carrying any historical emotional baggage with this person. It will not be a resourceful, transparent process if you come from a starting point of resentment and blame, or if the other person does. It is not a chance to let rip at your partner, mother or friends, releasing every little thing that has been bothering you.

Watch for any judgements, assumptions or stories within your language and phrase your words in a positive context.

- ♡ Don't dig up past problems or mistakes.
- ♡ Don't use words such as "ought to" or "should".
- ♡ Don't make it a list of all the things he or she is not doing or has not done.

- ♡ Do examine the exercise from an awareness of **compas-sion and curiosity to hear the other person's point of view.**
- ♡ Do acknowledge up front any contribution you may have made to the situation.
- ♡ Do listen to and hear what they say.

OK, we're ready for the exercise itself. Choose the key relationships in your life as a mum; they may be your own mum or mother-in-law, your nanny, your best friend, your father, your partner or husband. Work through this exercise with each of them separately. For these special people you are going to raise your and their awareness about the reality of the relationship and your expectations.

Step One: Where are we?
In one sentence, write down:
♡ Where do I believe our relationship is right now?
(Use no more than about 10 to 12 words.)

Share what you have written with each other and hear what the other person thinks. Both remain open to hearing each other's feelings. Watch and listen to the reaction of your inner voice, stay aware of unresourceful feelings and attempt to remain compassionate with and curious about each other. If you feel strong emotions, share them. You may need a break to reflect and compose yourself, then start to explain to each other why you feel the way you do.

Step Two: How are we meeting each other's needs?
♡ I feel the division of labour between us both financially and with our to-do tasks is...

♡ I feel supported in these areas... (list)

♡ I feel you could give me more support in these areas... (list)

♡ I didn't realise you would do so much... (either positive or negative, e.g. watching TV or working around the house)

♡ I thought you would do more of this...

♡ I believe that our shared approach to the children is...

Again, work through your feelings alone and then share your answers together. Where possible, discuss both people's views.

Step Three: How are we doing emotionally?
♡ The things I feel I can talk to you about are...

♡ The things I find it challenging to talk to you about are...

♡ I trust you implicitly with...

♡ I worry sometimes about you in these areas...

As before, work through your feelings alone and then share your answers together. Where possible, discuss both people's views.

Step Four: How am I doing?
♡ I think I am brilliant at...

♡ I would really like your help with...

Once more, work through your feelings alone and then share your answers together. Where possible, discuss both people's views.

I can only know from my own experience and that of the mums I have shared this tool with so far that the discussions in this exercise could have taken you to a new level of awareness, shared expectation and shared goals, or a place of reflection and the acknowledgement that further conversations need to be had. One thing I have observed is that the courage it takes to have these discussions is a strength that your children will observe in you, equipping them with a role model of courage, awareness and honest communication.

Following these discussions, decide together on the key areas that you would both like to improve and work on together. Go through the following task-based expectations audit, and agree times and dates to revisit either exercise.

EXERCISE 27
TASK-BASED EXPECTATIONS AUDIT

This really can be fun! Enter into it with the attitude of how fascinating it can be and laugh at how differently you see things. If you don't and you are like most families, you may just cry!

(There is a full A4 version available on my website, www.theonlymum.com.)

Give this list to the people around you to complete, then compare and discuss the answers.

Who is responsible for what?

CHILDREN				
	Me	You	Other person	Would like to discuss
Night duty				
Weekly activity planning				
School commitments (incl. covering sick days)				
Discipline				
Play dates				

CHILDREN				
	Me	You	Other person	Would like to discuss
Weekend activity planning				
Family holidays				
Add your own				
RELATIONSHIP				
Contraception				
Arranging one-on-one dates				
Meeting friends				
Initiating romance				
Initiating intimacy				

UNDERSTANDING WHO YOU ARE

RELATIONSHIP				
	Me	You	Other person	Would like to discuss
Add your own				
HOUSEHOLD CHORES				
Grocery shopping				
Meal planning				
Meal preparation				
Cleaning up after meals				
Laundry				
Ironing				
Tidying up				

HOUSEHOLD CHORES				
	Me	You	Other person	Would like to discuss
Hoovering				
Add your own				
ADMINISTRATION AND FINANCES				
Bringing income into the home				
Paying bills – household				
Paying bills – vehicles and possessions				
Savings and pension planning				
Add your own				

Finally discuss together:

♡ How will we talk about the other person not carrying out what they have agreed to do?

This is very important. It's all very well agreeing who will do what, but it is when something is not done that the compassion and understanding have to come in.

♡ Who is responsible for talking through the expectations of the other people listed in our expectations? That is, if grandma is responsible for something, does she know?

When it's done and you are both happy, celebrate!

MINDSET IN A MINUTE
UNDERSTANDING WHO YOU ARE

Be clear of your own personal values, look at the list on pages 115–16 and list your top three. See how many things you do every day which sit within your chosen values?

Be clear about what the inter-fear-ances are in your life.

Ask yourself: What is stopping me from being the person I truly want to be? What am I afraid of? What am I afraid that I cannot do?

Remember, FEAR is often False Evidence Appearing Real.

Clarify which fears and worries are ones you can actually do something about, take control of those and soon the others will seem smaller.

Happiness is good not only for your physical health, but your mental health too:

♡ Find something every day which makes you laugh.
♡ Smile at strangers in the supermarket or at work – not only will it make them feel good, it will you too!
♡ When you are feeling low write a gratitude list. Put down everything in your life that you are grateful for. I guarantee you will start to feel better as soon as you reflect on all you have written.
♡ Seek out people who make you feel good about you and the people and things you love. Spend your time with them, not people that you feel inadequate, unconfident or in awe of, not people you can't be yourself with.

♡ Treasure those special people who make you feel special and make time for them – they bring you health and happiness, as you will to them.

Undertake the exercise of the wheel of life. See what balance or lack of it there is in your life for the things that matter the most to you. Sit back and reflect on it and what it is telling you and ask yourself if you want anything to change.

Clarify the reality of your world both to you and those around you. Clarify expectations and roles, clear up any confusion so you can move forward aware of what is required. Understand the picture that both you and those around you have of a mum, and how you all see you in comparison to that picture.

If nothing else, start to accept that you are doing an OK job, you are a great mum who does her best most of the time. This is the absolute most that we or our children or would ask.

Undertake the expectation audit in this chapter, alone if necessary, just to highlight the areas of potential misunderstanding with those around you regarding the basic tasks you all do every day, then discuss them with the relevant people.

CHAPTER 5

LEARNING RESPONSE-ABILITY

Your life is the sum result of all the choices you make, both consciously and unconsciously. If you can control the process of choosing, you can control all aspects of your life. You can find the freedom that comes from being in charge of yourself. —Robert F Bennett

Everything you have learnt so far has taken you on a journey of discovery of both yourself and the people around you. It would be amazing if just looking at and understanding the reality of your world could take you to where you want to be in your life. But hey, I'm sorry; you actually have to do something! Building self-awareness and an understanding of yourself is essential, but now you actually have to stand up and be counted.

Here's the one bit of this book that you can't skip, skim through or ignore... The next stage on your journey is accepting that you're completely responsible for yourself and realising that no one is coming to the rescue. There's very little that you cannot do or have after you accept that:

If it's to be, it's up to me!

The reality is that learning responsibility involves three big steps:

1. Taking personal responsibility.
2. Improving your personal response-ability.
3. Setting your future goals and taking responsibility for making them happen.

TAKING PERSONAL RESPONSIBILITY

The chances are that right now you are neither perfectly happy nor completely unhappy, as most of us most of the time lie somewhere in between. If your conclusions from reading and completing the exercises so far are that you're not satisfied with your life, now is the time to do something about it.

If you continue to do the same things you have always done, everything will remain the same.

Is that OK?

If not, here's the truth:

Your life now is not the result of your genes, parents, kids, education, job, luck, timing, health, environment, horrendous events, disability, bullying or any other factor you may want to blame.

It is the choices you have made and the actions you have taken because of or in spite of the above that have brought you to where you are today.

Ouch!

For some of you this may be a hard truth to hear. In fact, hearing it may be just too painful right now, or even at any time. I resisted it for many years. I would never have chosen some of the painful events I have faced in my life and I felt powerless to be anything other than a victim of them. Only by realising that many years later, those events and that pain were still creating the person I was, and that I wasn't happy as her, more so that I did not want my children to live like her, did I feel brave enough to do something about it.

Are you still carrying the results of negative events that have happened to you over the years, letting them sculpt who you are now?

Would you like to put them down and leave them behind, walking forward from here free of any burdens that you really no longer need? It is totally possible and amazingly simple:

Change your choices and actions, take responsibility, and you will change the results that follow.

Only you know whether you have a choice to make.

Are you ready to put down your past hurts, your past inter-fear-ances, your past baggage?

EXERCISE 28
WHAT IS YOUR BAGGAGE?

You need a real leap of self-analysis here. Listen hard to your inner voice and write down what you hear.

Ask yourself the following questions:

♡ What are the events I consciously or unconsciously use as the reasons I have not achieved my potential?

♡ What effect do I believe they have had on me?

♡ Do I still carry the effects from them with me today?

♡ Do I want to carry the effects of these events with me for the rest of my life?

If yes, accept that and take responsibility alongside them. If not, leave them behind. (As always, if you need help with that, seek it.)

OK, deep breath, here goes... "I accept that these events are a part of me, my past, my journey. I thank them for any positives they brought me, and from here I move on without them."

WHAT IS RESPONSE-ABILITY?

This is the simplest lesson I have to share with you. It overwrites disappointment, frustration, anger, guilt, stress and pain. It is achingly simple and blindingly obvious. It is this:

Whatever is happening in our lives, or our children's lives, we *always* have the power to choose how we respond to any situation. We can stop life happening to us by taking *response-ability* for the choices we make.

The fact that we can build an ability to respond is not just my Pollyanna-inspired, airy-fairy theory, it has been proved and reinforced time and time again in the worst of situations.

In *Man's Search for Meaning* by Viktor Frankl, an amazingly humbling autobiographical account of a Jewish psychiatrist's experiences living for years in concentration camps, the least harsh of his words were: "The prisoners faced horrible undernourishment whilst having to do hard manual labour for 12 hours a day. In winter, this would mostly be in sub-zero temperatures, yet they didn't have any winter clothes. They were threatened by death daily and hourly. And they had no news of their loved ones, who had either been sent to another camp or gassed immediately." Frankl's parents, brother and pregnant wife all lost their lives. As you would expect, the survival rate was very low – only 1 in 28 survived.

Frankl believed: "He [who] knows the 'why' for his existence... will be able to bear almost any 'how'." He discovered that even through all the atrocities he and others faced, three things kept him alive: his love for his wife, his work (the need to share what he was learning) and his views on suffering. He talked about "spiritual freedom", which in essence is our absolute ability to choose which attitude we

186

have to things. Frankl realised that we can choose which attitude to take to suffering.

He and others in the camp could actually find mental freedom by realising that they always had the right to choose their response. In fact, they had more ability to do so than the soldiers running the camp, who were carrying out orders that they believed they could not have any control over.

I can't know what your life has brought you so far, nor do you of me, but I know that if these men could choose to take mental responsibility as they survived the worst atrocities known to humankind, it is possible for anyone.

Quite simply, if your life has meaning and purpose, you can meet the simplest human need to move forward, grow and work towards greater self-esteem by learning to choose how you respond to everything life and being a mum can bring.

I know I am making it sound simple – and yes, I do very much live in the real world – but it truly can be done, even in the darkest moments. I will show you how.

IMPROVING YOUR RESPONSE-ABILITY

It's Saturday morning, you wake up naturally, the sun is shining – it's a beautiful day, and you actually have no work to do. You can hear your partner downstairs brewing fresh coffee and the kids playing and laughing happily together. There is a note on the pillow saying:

Lie in, darling, we know how hard you work, just relax. I'm taking the kids swimming and will give them lunch out. The morning is yours.

You walk through to the bathroom and the scales say you have lost 2kg this week. As you luxuriate in a deep bath, getting time finally to tackle the overgrowth of stubble on your legs, you hear the family heading out. Scented and smooth, you saunter downstairs, to see hot croissants and coffee waiting for you and a selection of magazines.

In my world I would call this a good day – actually I'd call it unbelievable, but that's another story. Good obviously means different things to different people, but in essence a good day is one when everything has gone your way. Realistically it would be the day that you actually got longer than four hours' solid sleep, your children wake up after the sun has risen, you manage to grab a five-second shower and the children are fed, dressed and fairly happy to get out for the school run. You have remembered lunches, sports kits and your mother's birthday, and your presentation is finished for today's meeting. Or your partner and kids have given you a big hug and thanks for all you do on their way out.

When was the last time you had a good day? Or even a good hour?

In contrast, how often do you get woken through the night with a selection of tummy aches, bad dreams, coughs or just inexplicable tears and a need to have "Mummy sleep with me"? You finally give in at 5 a.m., stumble through breakfast where every food is refused, face hysterics about not wanting to go to school, your husband's furious at losing his car keys and you find that your maternity trousers are not only the cleanest item in your wardrobe but also the closest thing to something that does up. Having parked seemingly three miles from school as you are too late for a space, you finally get there to find it's a fancy dress day and you totally forgot. Mortified with guilt, you send your poor uniformed children in surrounded by Cinderellas, Buzz Lightyears and Batmen. (Yes, I have done this.) Then to top it all you are late for your first appoint-ment that morning.

For those of us who work, it is the 8 a.m. call from your childcare to say there is a problem, or even worse the 11 a.m. call to say your child is poorly and needs their mum when you are just heading in for a crucial meeting. Or the client call that runs over, meaning you know you will be the last mum at school pick-up and your child will look at you with sad eyes again.

For both of these days I am listing a series of events that have happened. But your personal rating of those events and how they subsequently affect you are down to your percep-tion. For example, waking to a sun-filled day could be a bad start for someone with pale skin and acute hayfever.

Let me illustrate this a bit more. Imagine starting your day on a high. The children are relaxed and happy and eat a good breakfast, you manage to grab a bite yourself and you are all off for your respective days. On the way out, you pick up a phone message from your partner, a request to call him immediately: "It is urgent." How quickly does your high start to diminish as he tells you he has to work late and can't get to your son's football match that afternoon, and that you will have to get the food shopping he said he would on your way home from work, requiring you to leave early... again. Also, sorry, but he won't be home in time for the children's bedtime. In seconds, events have dropped your day from a high to a self-perceived lower point on the scale.

Now imagine that as you come off the phone your tod-dler spills her blackcurrant drink all over herself and is wet and tearful, on a day when you don't have any clean clothes. My guess is that your reaction to the accidental spillage would be completely different had you not had that phone call.

On a good day spillages can be a slight hump, easily overcome with cuddles and a calm reassurance that drinking is a learning curve and your child is improving at their own speed. On a challenging day they are carelessness, stupidity or just plain naughtiness, requiring or rather reacted to with annoyance, impatience and maybe even punishment.

What this demonstrates is that events create a resourceful or unresourceful set of emotions. This emotional state can then have an impact on your response to the next event that occurs, forming a spiral of events where how you respond is influenced by how you feel as a result of the previous occurrence. What is important is that the way you respond in the moment has a long-term impact on both yourself and your children.

When I was on my diet rollercoaster post-baby, I would be known to float through a day when I felt I had lost weight. Stressed husband, moaning children, washing machine breakdowns, lost teddy bear – everything was taken in my stride and I remained calm and contented. A week later, at the same weight, I could be trudging through my day, feeling fat and unhappy as I hadn't lost any weight. I'd be impatient, grumpy with my children and snapping at the world. All that had changed was my perception and my chosen (or rather unconscious) response to the same event, the same weight.

This is the key.

There are many events that can threaten to move us up and down the scale of emotions. The feeling of being out of control is one of the biggest reasons given to doctors and counsellors for feeling overwhelmed as a parent. Controlling how we respond is therefore a start to lessening the feelings that can lead to that state of being overwhelmed.

THE WORST OF TIMES

I am well aware that there are events we have no control over, especially when it comes to bringing up children. I also know from very personal experience, and those of some of the amazing mums I have met, that at times life as a mum can be hard and heartbreaking. Soon after his birth, my youngest son was repeatedly rushed into hospital with frightening complications from an illness he had from birth, only to contract meningitis. I am acutely aware that the seconds, minutes, hours sat next to your child not knowing if they will live lead to a level of heartache no parent should have to feel. When their screams of pain cannot be comforted and there is nothing you can do, your mind runs scenarios and pictures of futures that are unbearably sad, mixed with the fear of not knowing how something will resolve itself. Sometimes there is nothing you can do to save your child, other than to trust in the medical staff and be there for your child and love them. My son survived and thrived, but there were parents on that high-dependency unit whose children didn't survive or who will spend a lifetime needing hospital care or living with extra challenges.

I can say, from my and their shared experiences, that keeping your response controlled and calibrating each new challenge in isolation, with a sense of hope, at least does not make the experience any worse and does help you be more able to cope and stay strong. As I discussed earlier in the book, I am not advocating ignoring pain and sadness – in fact just the opposite, listening to emotions is essential for mental wellbeing – but when your child needs your strength, this technique can find you emotional stability and a feeling that you are achieving something when all else fails.

IMPROVING YOUR ABILITY TO CHOOSE YOUR RESPONSE

You can make a choice to respond to an event based on the feelings from a previous event, or to start having an awareness of your emotional state, taking responsibility for how you feel and treating each event separately.

The one thing you can have *complete* control over is your response to every event. You can choose whether its effect will last beyond the event itself. This is your first step to having responsibility for your actions.

Start becoming aware of how each conversation, interaction with your children or challenge from your day starts to affect your mood and how you then view or respond to the next event. In essence, this is a mental checking-in procedure.

Say the day starts with a 5 a.m. tantrum from one child, following a night of teething and screaming from another. You could spend the rest of the day resentful, frustrated and fed up that you only got three hours' sleep, which would ensure that everyone, including you, has a terrible day.

Or you could check in with your response to your lack of sleep, realise that you have started the day on a low and try to mentally restore yourself to a higher baseline or make sure you plan something into your day that you can look forward to, so your mood will pick up. It could be a cup of proper coffee, a quick telephone conversation with a good friend, or just asking your partner to let you watch your favourite programme on TV that evening. You're consciously choosing not to let a bad event cause a bad day.

You are taking responsibility.

It's that simple!

Well almost. Let me just clarify a point that frequently comes up in my workshops. I want to share the example of one mum who has two teenage boys.

One of her sons has left his bedroom in a tip *again*, including wet towels, plates, glasses... Her immediate reaction in the past has been either:

1   Go completely mad *again*, feel frustrated, angry, shout a lot while clearing up the mess.
2   Go completely mad and 'force' son to clear up, ultimately having a massive row *again* (in her words: "At least you feel some satisfaction that he 'learned' he will have to clear up").

She worried that taking response-ability could mean:

3   Avoid the arguments and just clear up. Don't go mad: "choose" to be calm and unaffected. After all, what are a few towels in the scheme of things?

Taking responsibility does not mean that you just do everything yourself that others don't do, or make everything right! It is not about merely correcting any event that has caused you stress. For this mum and others this caused some doubt, as she had a nagging voice telling her: "I have relinquished my position. Yes, I am calmer and have chosen not to go through the anxiety of rage, but at what cost has this been achieved? I've had to forgo my power base and it makes me seem weak."

The role of the response-ability model is only to alter the level of resourcefulness with which you respond to a stressful event. It allows you to find a way of communicating your feelings and needs resourcefully and making a request accordingly. The reality may be that this "lesson" you believe is essential for your child may never be learned. You either

193

choose to accept that reality, try to make a request resourcefully, or keep repeating the pain of the discord between your child and you. For many mums, knowing that you communicated your request clearly and with a level of resourcefulness that brought you no further optional suffering is enough to accept reality as it is. For some this is one of the realities of being a mum that is hardest of all to accept. A lesson we see as essential for our children, no matter how brilliantly we teach it (in our own perception), may never be learnt. That is our children's choice.

Is there a place for winning and losing in parenting? That is your personal decision.

The perception of holding a position on a discussion is covered over the next few pages, so for those of you who like to win and get what you want in your relationships, even those with your family, by defeating others, read on...

For now, ponder the thought: is strength being open and aware to someone else's reality and finding peace with that, or is it holding on fast to your beliefs and closing your eyes to any other version of reality than yours?

Remember the equation:

$$E+S+R=O$$

A perceived challenging Event + the context from its Story + your chosen Response = your Outcome

Simply put, by choosing how you respond to each event in your life:

- ♡ Assessing its impact in isolation
- ♡ Removing judgements
- ♡ Examining your underlying feelings
- ♡ Realising your needs, stories and values

194

you can achieve the most resourceful state to achieve your realistic outcome (maybe not your ideal outcome, since we're still living in the real world!).

EXERCISE 29
CHOOSING HOW YOU FEEL

Today, as life happens around you, start observing how events are making you feel.

Ask yourself what you are feeling about the effects of each event and how you are transferring or carrying those feelings into your conversations and interactions with your children and others around you.

♡ Does a perceived bad event have to mean facing the rest of the day feeling unresourceful?

♡ Do you need to end another day feeling stressed, not only at the world and your family but at yourself as well?

Isolate the bad events as one-offs and start viewing each new event in its own context.

Build your level of self-awareness about how you respond and carry your responses forward.

The good news is that you have a choice. The bad news is that if you react negatively to a first-level stressor, compose a PLOM or a negative story, climb up your ladder of inference and react, creating more negative outcomes, you can really quickly fall into a vicious cycle. Believe me, it can only take seconds and once you start falling the day can be really hard to retrieve.

HOW DO I CHOOSE MY RESPONSE IN THE MIDST OF A REAL-LIFE DAY?

Believe me, I do live in a world of tantrums, vomiting, hair pulling, biting, food throwing, poo smearing, clients needing my call back, emails to catch up on – although not yet the underage sex, drunkenness, drug taking and all the potential future elements of a real-world mum's life.

So the bottom line is that there are two truths you need to bear in mind.

Sometimes you just can't choose
First, often you won't choose your response.

No caveats, no blame, no expectations – you could practise A TRUTH for 50 years and still be triggered by the child-led challenges your life will bring. Sometimes you will, in the moment, react negatively. It's a fact, accept it.

What you can do is take responsibility, after your instant reaction. When you are able to emotionally, take the actions that you know are necessary. Apologise if you feel the reaction requires it, both to the person you reacted to and, importantly, to your children. This is a great opportunity to model your ability to make mistakes and learn from them and to show them that we are always learning and that saying sorry is part of taking responsibility and growing.

Maybe say, "Mummy reacted to ... in a way I feel sad about and I want to apologise to you. It wasn't behaviour I'm proud of and I will try my best to act differently the next time."

Surely that's what you're asking of them, isn't it?

Apologise to yourself as well if you feel you need to: "I reacted to that, I didn't choose my response, that's the reality of what happened. I accept it, and do you know what, I am sorry."

196

Big reminder: Guilt, shame and regret are always, always, always based on stories, jumps up your ladder or unhelpful inner critic punishment of what should have been. When you feel these emotions, whatever the "crime", forgive yourself, learn from them and move on.

Sarah had grown up in a very strict family where rules were enforced with physical punishment. She was adamant that she would bring her children up differently and she was absolutely against physical punishment towards children. When her second child, a daughter, was born, her eldest child, only 4 at the time, took the new addition to the family really badly. He created diversions at every opportunity when Sarah had to do things with his baby sister and then, when his sister was 10 months old, he whacked her with a toy as she tried to take it from him.

Without a thought, in a split second, Sarah totally lost her temper with her son, yanked him by the arm off the floor and slapped him. He was hysterical, the baby was screaming and Sarah was instantly and completely horrified and devastated by what she had done.

She held her son and daughter tightly, crying at what she had done to them and to herself. She carried a sense of shame, guilt, remorse and regret with her for the whole day.

With a new-found awareness of responsibility, she mentally sought out self-acceptance over the day. At bedtime, she sat her son and daughter down, held them both tightly and talked them through what had happened.

She shared how sad she was, how she did not believe that what she had done was right, and that she would like to say sorry. Her son looked up at her and said, "Mumma we all make mistakes, that's what you always tell me, don't be sad..."

When she shakily shared this story with me, she still felt devastated, but knew she had, as soon as she could, taken responsibility. Although she felt that by no means excused her behaviour, it did stop it from being unbearable to live with.

Her children may remember her anger, but they would also connect that anger with her sadness and her apology.

Before I get inundated by hundreds of angry emails claiming that I am condoning violence to children, I am not. I am just not judging another mum who is also endeavouring to do her best. If you can sit reading this book and tell me that you have never, never reacted to your child with anger, either snapping, shouting or simply ignoring your child, then maybe you can sit in judgement of Sarah. However, you did not grow up with the lessons and examples from childhood that Sarah did, you did not walk in her shoes. Until you or I have, all we can see is her ability to atone, learn from and change any reactions she had.

So even when you react in the worst ways, you can still take responsibility, even after the event. Similarly, if you do react in a way that you are sad about, however bad it may be, do something about it.

It's FAB!
The second truth is the mum's life saver:

FAB!

I say this with a broad 1980s, two-thumbs-up kid's grin, knowing that FAB was the very best my teenage mind could imagine.

If you gain nothing else from this book let it be this, the ultimate tool in the A TRUTH toolbox, the one thing that you must always carry with you and something that will stop you in your tracks in the worst of moments – the FAB response.

It was created by my husband Alec Grimsley, the author of *Vital Conversations*, who is as much a mum for my boys as I am at times and has handled our workload full time as I met work deadlines. It stands for:

Fascinating
Acknowledge
Breathe

Picture this:

It's teatime. You've had a hell of a day, a real mess of tears, tantrums, moody teenagers or petulant tots, storming out or foot stamping. The TV broke down, the delivery you stayed in all morning for arrived 30 seconds after you'd left for the school run, only to sit out in the rain until you returned. You were late for everything and you are full of a cold. Your beautiful, chubby-faced, 3-year-old angel decides to throw her plate of freshly prepared food all over you, the floor, the walls and her sister. Chaos ensues.

This is when the FAB response comes into its own.

Step 1: Stop and silently and with irony say "Fascinating!" to yourself. If the mood takes you it could be prefixed with any other f... word that brings a smile to your face.

I know this sounds completely ridiculous, but it works. In psychological terms it's a pattern breaker or interrupter. It's a method often used when people experience panic or anxiety – the word halts a pathway of thought, and in this case a reaction, in its tracks. The irony makes you smile every time. If the word"fascinating" doesn't work for you, choose another word, maybe "interesting"," curious" or "golly gosh"!

Saying it takes seconds, but in about 8 out of 10 cases it will pull you out of your habitual pattern of reaction.

Then take the other two steps of the FAB response:

Step 2: Acknowledge to yourself how the event is making you feel, hear and listen to your exasperation, annoyance, frustration or sadness.

Step 3: Breathe. Take two deep breaths, counting in for 6 and counting out for 6 (that is, breaths where your stomach actually extends as you breathe, filling your lungs with a fresh source of air).

OK, now smile at or have serious words with your giggling daughter as you see fit, clean her and everything else up and find her something else to eat.

Regardless of your story, where you are on your ladder, whatever inter-fear-ance you are experiencing, whatever your unmet needs, thoughts or feelings, this simple 30-second activity will take you further on your journey of response-ability than any other.

Go on, give it a try...

TAKING RESPONSIBILITY FOR HOW YOU COMMUNICATE

"How would you ask?" I say this to my 3 year old all the time, hoping that this not very subtle reminder will gently instil in him the need to say "please" before he requests anything. Only after six months of sounding like a stuck record did a friend recommend that I give him a good reason for why "please" matters. I talked him through the importance of valuing other people's actions and letting them know that we appreciate what they are doing for us. I still don't get a "please" every time, but I do see him considering and adding a "please" with understanding rather than because he thinks he needs to to get what he wants.

Asking for things or making a request is no different for adults. We can unconsciously become very poor at translating our needs into clear requests to those around us.

For example, how often do you say "I'm thirsty" when you would like someone to make you a drink?

Ali and her husband Steve were sat one evening chatting through their day. Ali slumped pointedly down on the sofa with a huge sigh and then she felt that she clearly listed what she had done all day, ending with what she felt she deserved, for him to make her a cup of tea.

What she said was: "I haven't stopped all day, the dog was sick, I forgot Josh's change of clothes for nursery and he peed all over himself. I had to do the supermarket shop and Zoe cried all the way around. We got soaked walking the dog in the rain, Zoe fell over and bumped her knee and then neither of them went off to sleep. I'm dying for a cuppa, are you busy?"

Steve interpreted this as: "I've had a busy day, are you busy?" He didn't hear a request for a cup of tea. He was busy, so he replied that he was and carried on with his work.

Ali felt that she had clearly stated her need for a cup of tea and that Steve had judged her need as unimportant. She allowed her need to be negated and made her own cup of tea, but felt resentful and angry towards him. This event was repeated day after day in their house.

Here begins one of the most useful lessons I have learnt on my journey of understanding communication. Just as we all paint a unique picture of the world and seek out the evidence to match that picture, we all have the potential to interpret verbal communication in myriad different ways.

For Ali, saying "I'm thirsty" was a clear request for a cup of tea, backed up with a wealth of explanation and justification as to why she believed her husband should make it. Her husband heard no such need or request.

Even when we have a clear picture of our needs and explanations and requirements for help, we have to translate and communicate them to the people around us in a language they can understand. This is about taking responsibility for the outcomes in our lives. How many times have you resented what someone has done wrong or hasn't done at all, and yet you had neither explained what your requirements and expectations were or what you would like the outcome to be.

Think of the number of times you have heard people say things like:

♡ "My God, are they stupid, they should just know."
♡ "I don't like to nag, but..."
♡ "They can see what I do, why can't they just do the same?"

The reality is that we all see life differently, and we all hear words differently.

People see the world through the story or picture they have created. They can never with intuition or guesswork know exactly what your picture of meeting your need looks like, unless you clearly explain it to them.

We can't expect others to know what we want, no matter how many years they have known us for, just as we can never truly picture what another human being wants without asking.

I am not excusing insensitivity, ignorance, lethargy or laziness on the part of others. What I am sharing is the basic human psychological fact that no one can guess what you want and get it right every time unless you clarify it.

Mums often tell me that they don't want to nag. Often the nagging sounds something like this: "Will you please stop leaving your coffee cup on the floor?"

The people around them hear that they are not to leave their coffee cup on the floor, so for a while at least they pick their cup up and leave it on the table in the lounge. The mum then moans that they have to keep nagging about a coffee cup left on the table.

When you actually analyse what the unmet need is here, it is often the need for support and for those around her to take responsibility for clearing up after themselves. As mad as it may sound to you, when you say "Will you please stop leaving your coffee cup on the floor?", others may not intuitively realise that this means "Pick it up and either wash it up or put it in the dishwasher". This is what it means to you, not them. They've taken the coffee cup off the floor, which is what you asked them to do.

Clearing up and putting a coffee cup away may be a small thing in someone else's world, something of little importance to them. To you it may represent your interpretation of how they support you, respect your role, share your responsibility. The only way others can clearly understand when their small actions have huge ramifications for us is when we share our needs when we ask them to do something. So you need to say instead:

> *John, keeping on top of things around the house and keeping the place tidy is really important to me, I work as many hours as you, so please would you pop your own coffee cup in the dishwasher when you are finished with it, as I find it disrespectful to me when you leave it on the floor.*

You may be thinking that if you have to share your needs and make a clear, specific request for everything anyone does for you, you will never get anything done and may as well give up now. This is where you have to choose your battles. There are actually very few actions that we interpret as a "red rag to a bull", that send us shooting up our ladder of inference and cause us to be emotionally hijacked. You just need to find out which ones are yours.

So the steps to making a clear request are these:

♡ Understand your underlying needs and interests (why are you making the request?).
♡ Be honest and transparent – share what you feel will meet your need.
♡ Ask with a focus on the positive (what you want).
♡ Use doable, action language (state the action that someone can take).
♡ Be specific and clear:
  Who you want to do what
  What you would like them to do
  When
  How long for etc.

It all sounds very formal, but take my word for it, when you actually start practising it, no one seems to notice the specificity and what you are asking for gets done, if the other person agrees to do it. If they do say no, don't go up your ladder and berate them or silently seethe, be curious and find out their reasons.

And just like my 3-year-old son, do say "please", which I often forget to do!

FLEXIBLE WORKING – REALLY?

One area of clarity about our needs that comes up repeatedly with mums who work is flexible working. Employers are starting to understand and value the massive contribution that back-to-work mums are making to our organisations. Many support services and programmes have been put in place by the more progressive employers. Yet I continuously hear laments from part-time workers. I have yet to meet a part-time working mum who works the hours she has agreed on paper with her employer.

Some of you accept this reality, are truly passionate about your role and just embrace the long working hours as part of you being the person you want to be. Many of you, however, are carrying an underlying weight of disillusion or resentment, either at your employer, your partner or yourself. This culminates in a deprecating self-talk of being a pushover, being taken advantage of, or just your employer taking the mickey. Being dissatisfied with this state of affairs will not only chip away at your mood, resourcefulness and energy levels, it will be reflected, as we know from our iceberg, in the results we achieve at work.

Employers are now far more aware that clear discussions of needs, and clear requests from employers, lead to both better results from mums who work and also happier, more resourceful employees.

EXERCISE 30
REQUESTING TO MEET YOUR NEEDS AT WORK

If you are a working mum, how do you feel about the hours you are working?

♡ For you does part time mean part time?

♡ Are the hours you are contracted to do and the benefits that they bring meeting your needs for your work?

♡ Are your partner, boss, childcare and children supporting you with the hours that you work?

♡ How much of the imbalance is down quite simply to you, your desire to succeed, your fears about falling behind, your need for a perfect house?

♡ What would you like to change in an ideal world?

♡ Are any of these ideas possible to change in your world?

♡ Could you request a discussion on them with the appropriate person?

DON'T SWEAT THE SMALL STUFF

Human beings inherently want to meet others' needs wherever possible when they don't cancel out our own. When given a clear explanation of expectations and a clear request for a desired outcome, most people will carry out the instructions with pleasure.

I am by no means advocating that you start issuing orders to everyone and that the people around you should start carrying them out. All I am advising is that you be clear about what actions by the people around you would meet your needs and expectations. They can choose whether to accept your request and there the communication begins.

This will stop the unacknowledged resentment, martyr-dom, victim and persecutor thoughts when you prevent your needs from being met.

IT IS A CRUEL WORLD

If there is anything that we wish to change in the child, we should first examine it and see whether it is not some-thing that could better be changed in ourselves.
—CG Jung, Integration of the Personality, 1939

One additional area to analyse is whether you view the world and the people around you as inherently good, want-ing to help, supportive and loving. Or is there a part of you that worries that people will meet their own self-interest first, that they are inherently prone to laziness, sloppy stan-dards and letting you down?

Your view may differ for different people around you, but the chances are, especially if you have circumnavigated the drama triangle we talked about in Chapter 3, that you have some emotional baggage and resentment in relation to some of the people around you. Over the course of many conversations or arguments, you may have built up a bank of feelings that could be clouding how you expect someone to react to your request. Often these feelings are written from the depths of a story or cycle of drama with that person.

Clarify for yourself any stories, negative thoughts or feelings you may have in your expectations of others before you make any request of them. If you do expect them to fail to fulfil your request, refuse to do it or be resentful and angry at being asked, ask yourself whether over time you could have contributed to how they feel.

Do you criticise them for carrying out your requests incorrectly? Have you given them something to do and then outwardly or by your behaviour belittled their actions?

Life, events and people's treatment of us can knock the spirit out of our souls. While not everyone is a wonderful person, the wish to grow as a human being is somewhere in all of us. When asked clearly and specifically, with a full explanation of what the task being completed means to you, I believe that most people who care about you will do their best to achieve it if they can.

Ask yourself whether you believe that too.

If you don't, what part did you play in that not being the case?

If you don't believe the people around you are positive, use the relationship audit at the end of Chapter 4 to work out why, before you start making requests.

Everything is in the mind. That's where it all starts. Knowing what you want is the first step towards getting it. —**Mae West**

WORKING OUT THE INTERESTS

Over the course of my career I have attended, delivered and written many development programmes on negotiation based on the idea of winning, getting others to do what you want them to do. I have taught everything from using covert scare tactics to subtle manipulation to get your needs met, a sale completed or a project finished.

I have chosen to supersede all of these as a mum, where the stakes are my personal relationships, my friends, my family, my reputation as a practitioner and, most importantly, the way my children learn to communicate based on what they observe from me. I have made the decision to find a way of communicating that comes from meeting all parties' needs as well as possible, from a core place of peace, not conflict or competition.

One communication tool I have found essential in making requests and then hearing and understanding the needs of the person you are asking is working from the level of each person's interests. Let me explain what I mean.

Helen and Paul have been married for 11 years and have argued for most of that time about having a window open at night in their room, or any room they spend the night in.

Helen claims to be unable to sleep without a window open. She feels stuffy and uncomfortable and wakes feeling groggy and grumpy if she isn't able to breathe fresh air. Paul needs silence to sleep well and is unable to get off to sleep with a window open, because he can't stop himself listening to the sounds from outside.

Their separate positions are:

Helen: Window open – sleep well.
Paul: Window closed – sleep well.

As sad as it sounds, this happily married couple started sleeping apart 10 years ago, one with the window open, the other with it closed, to meet both of their needs.

When asked to think about their underlying needs and interests in relation to the window, they managed to see an alternative that allowed them to share their room again.

Helen's interest: her need for fresh air.
Paul's interest: his need for a quiet room to sleep in.

To meet both their interests, they purchased some very effective ear plugs that Paul could hook in as they settled to sleep (they both found this completely hilarious, which helped ease the tension). The caveat was that Helen could wake him up if she needed his help with the children, since he could no longer hear them cry. They now share a room and all the benefits that brings again.

If you hit a stalemate in a discussion or when making requests, clarify for yourself what your underlying interest is, and where possible ask the person you are communicating with to do the same. Ask:

♡ "What is important to you about this?"
♡ "What would having/doing this give you?

Three examples:

If you are asking your 18-year-old daughter not to be out late, her interest may be that all her friends stay out until the early hours, so why shouldn't she?

Encourage her to share your interest as a mum: "I have a need for your safety and for my peace of mind. My interest is for me to know before I go to sleep that you are home and safe. How can we meet that need as well as your needs and interests?"

Inshi and her partner both worked full time, their son was in childcare full time, and they in theory had agreed to share the pick-up and drop-off times. In reality Inshi's partner had only managed to pick up their son twice throughout the last school term, meaning that Inshi had left work early every day, a fact that had been brought up by her line manager.

Her partner's position was that he was the main breadwinner and in his competitive sales environment leaving early regularly was an impossibility.

Inshi's position was that she earned almost as much as him, that her money greatly contributed to the lifestyle they enjoyed and that she was now putting her career in jeopardy by continuously leaving early.

Once they examined their interests, they agreed to pay one of the fellow mums to pick up their son three days a week and they each proactively arranged one day a week where they could start earlier and leave to pick up their son. Both felt that their interests and those of their son had been met, fairly.

Two parents were discussing the school they were going to send their son to. The mother wanted him to go to the nearest fee-paying school, the father felt that the local school was fine, they had both had a state education and it was good enough for them and so would be for their son.

On examination their interests were:

Mum: for their son to get the best start in life with his education, even if that had financial implications for them.

Dad: for their son to get the best start in life with his education, without adding an extra burden to his already stretched financial contributions.

They agreed that as the mother felt so strongly, she would return to work to fund the school fees. Another interest-based conclusion may have been for the mum to become heavily involved in the local school as a governor or teacher's assistant and play an active part in supporting her son's education.

So when making a request, or when having a discussion that seems to have reached a dead end, step back and work out what both parties' feelings, needs and interests are. There may be a solution hidden beneath the surface which works for everybody.

YOU WON'T GET IT RIGHT ALL THE TIME

Taking responsibility, improving your response-ability and communicating your needs and requests effectively take a lifetime to get right. And no one gets it right all the time. New contexts and traumatic events will take your breath away and your ability to respond resourcefully will disappear.

But in the process of growing rather than decaying, what counts is that you keep trying. As soon as you are mentally capable, take up the responsibility again. You can never ask more of yourself than that.

WHAT IS A GOOD MUM?

You have undertaken a journey to become more self-aware, to get to know your inner voice, what you are feeling, what you need and the stories that your emotions originate from. You have made the choice to accept responsibility and own your contribution to where you are now and have decided to take a path of greater responsibility as you move forward.

Before we look at the last part of A TRUTH, let's go right back to the beginning. I am going to ask you to revisit the first questions you asked yourself about being a mum.

EXERCISE 31
ARE YOU A GOOD ENOUGH MUM?

Now that you've read this far in the book, what do you now believe, for you, makes a good mum?

What character traits would she have?

How would a great mum feel about herself?

Are you a good enough mum?

If you feel you may not be, check out any stories you are still holding on to and ask yourself for acceptance of where you are.

Do you think you can be your idea of a good mum?

Phew... we have come full circle. You have established the gap between what you believe being a good mum looks like and where you are.

You will have absorbed from your reading that the way we act comes from the way we think, and that we have the ability to ensure that we make those actions resourceful. You have examined and assessed your inner self and seen what you are made of, you have analysed and assessed your relationships and your communication. You may have surprised or even shocked yourself, and you will have opened many discussions either with yourself or others that have brought you further insight.

213

But you can't just tick the box called self-awareness and responsibility and leave it there. Like me, you now have a choice every day about how you go forward with your new-found understanding.

Your children will have learnt alongside you, observing your confidence, fears, doubts and learning. They will have watched their mum make mistakes, use the word "fascinating" more times than any other and aim to live with courage and conviction.

Two final elements will seal your new-found knowledge. You are going to make a plan of action, which I talk about in the interlude, and then you're going to tackle the final stage of A TRUTH, making these new ways of thinking habitual.

GOAL SETTING

A person is only as big as the dream they dare to live.

At this point you could put the book down, feel good at having gained some self-awareness and self-acceptance of yourself as a mum and get on with your life. But if you did, you'd be missing out on your full potential.

The rest of the book requires you to think, reflect, brainstorm, plan and most importantly take action. It is showing you how to start your life plan and it will require time and effort!

No one would build a house without a set of plans, yet most mums (or anyone for that matter) rarely consider developing a plan for their life. Do you feel your life is as important as a house? If you do, then it's time to start your life planning.

> *If you don't design your own life plan, chances are you'll fall into someone else's plan. And guess what they have planned for you? Not much!* —**Jim Rohn**

THE GAP BETWEEN CURRENT STATE AND DESIRED STATE

At the very start of the book we established that as mums, unlike when we're at work, we tend to head through our days with no objectives to meet, no job description to fulfil, no feedback and no reward. Well, now we're going to change that!

This is your chance to acknowledge, plan and take action to close the gap between how you are now and your

215

desired state, moving forward what you would ideally like to change, maintain, improve or build on in certain key areas of your life.

When you completed the wheel of life exercise on page 143, you were describing your current state, your present reality. There might well be parts of your life where your reality is fantastic, but other aspects like health, finances or your relationship might not be working so well.

Before I start looking at how you can close that gap, it's crucial that your life plan and the goals you wish to pursue are becoming truly aligned, so I need to ask you to reconnect with some of the earlier work you did on yourself. You're going to revisit three exercises from earlier in the book and use these personal insights as the raw material from which to create your new life plan and key goals.

I can't be sat next to you as you write your plans for the future, so I am going to try to include all the elements that other mums have encountered when trying to reach their goals. However, if you do want any further help, support, a full template or examples of other people's life plans, look on the website, www.theonlymum.com.

You are now the project manager on a brand new account, "Project You". This is your plan for your future as you would like to see it.

The significance of a man is not in what he attains but in what he longs to attain. —**Kahlil Gibran**

First, go back to Exercises 13 and 15, where you set your values, both as a mum and as a family. Reappraise those values and ask yourself if they are still the core of who you are and want to be in the future.

Secondly, re-evaluate your wheel of life in Exercise 20 and look at where the gaps currently are between your hopes in each of those areas and where you are now. What would you like to change on that wheel?

Finally, review Exercise 3 at the start of the book where you are floating above your funeral and listening to what your children and other loved ones are saying about you. What did that exercise inspire you to change?

Use the boxes below to transfer your answers from the previous exercises

Core values:

```
[                                                         ]
```

Wheel of life: What areas are you most motivated to address?

```
[                                                         ]
```

Funeral testimonials: What would you like your friends, family and children to say about you, your qualities and what you achieved?

```
[                                                         ]
```

BUILDING YOUR GAP MUSCLES

Before you go any further, it doesn't matter whether you use a five-page template from my website or the back of your shopping list pad to write your life plan, only two things truly matter:

♡ It must inspire and motivate you.
♡ You must include some goals that will bring you some quick wins to build your confidence and some that right now feel virtually impossible.

My belief is that writing the plan is something most of us could do, maybe have done before, and it can look great in the journal or file we store it in... for years. Making your plan a reality and achieving your goals requires the right mindset strategies to start building your belief, confidence and competence. This is what I call the Goal Achievement Process or GAP.

If I can help you to achieve one small goal, that achievement will build a little more self-belief and confidence in your ability to stay focused and disciplined. You may also find that your levels of personal resilience and resourcefulness are now at a point where you can take on an even more important and challenging goal or life change.

EXERCISE 32
CHOOSE YOUR FIRST THREE GOALS

Take a little time now to think of three goals that if you achieved them would make a positive difference to your life.
Write them here:

1

2

3

Choose at least one goal that you could achieve in the next 1–6 months. Your second goal might be more challenging and require a longer-term view for its final accomplishment, say 6–18 months. The final goal can be medium or long term, as you wish.

If you have never set a goal before it's hard to know where to start, but if you consider once more the wheel of life and what key areas you want to make improvements in, you can begin to come up with potential goals that move you from your current state to the desired state you are looking for in that area.

Here are a few examples of short- to medium-term goals from women I have shared this process with:

Finding two hours per week of "me time" (no kids, just time solely for me).
Going back to college to study or upgrade key skills.

219

Getting a new job or changing career.
Having weekly dates with my partner to rekindle the romance.
Finding a sport or type of exercise programme that I enjoy.
Finding new friends.
Organising a holiday to somewhere a little more adventurous.
Taking more pride in and better care of my appearance.

Clarify with yourself that these are your true goals, that they are coming from your soul, not the goals that you believe others would want from you. True success in achieving your goals comes from being aware of and honest about what you truly want. Your goals may not be noble, spiritual or inspirational, but they must be true to you.

If some of these areas, such as finances, are partly dependent on your partner or others (maybe acceptance into university, a subsequent pregnancy, overcoming a health issue), then word them in a way that accepts what you can control or influence and set that as your goal. If applicable, seek out and discuss how other people involved in your goal see it, or make it a goal to go and find out. You never know if you don't at least try.

If you're having difficulty, just come up with one goal and write it in the box. Don't worry too much about how you're going to do it, but do describe why it's important to you and answer the other questions in the box.

GOAL:

Why is it important that you achieve this goal?

What will you get if you achieve it?

What will it cost you if you don't?

GO OUT ON THE RAS

At this point I am going to share with you a mindset difference that will make a difference for you:

"Everyone is pregnant!"

I don't know your fertility or pregnancy history and I won't
bore you with mine, but to demonstrate the point, I am
going to ask you to think back to when you first realised
you would like to have a baby or you started trying for one.
Suddenly, on your radar what did every female under the
age of 60 seem to be?

Either pregnant or a mum with beautiful, well-behaved
kids! I'm sure you realise that there wasn't a sudden fertility

221

surge, it was just that before being pregnant mattered to you, you didn't have a strong mental association with it.

What's happening is that a part of your brain called the reticular activating system or RAS is put into action. This works at an unconscious level. When you become focused on a particular thing, having a baby for example, the RAS acts like a mental peripheral vision or radar. When it spots the things that you consider important and relevant, it throws them into your conscious mind and you notice them.

Have you ever thought vaguely about signing up to a gym, doing yoga or taking a class in something and then coincidentally that day an advert for the thing you want to do seems to leap off the page of the local magazine or paper you're reading? You are having doubts and worries about being a working mum and suddenly every article in your paper and on the news is telling you the negative effects of working on your children. That is the RAS filtering for what you want.

What's all this got to do with achieving goals? The RAS is continually searching out the resources that you need. If you set a specific goal to eat more healthily – for example, "I will eat low-fat food, with less than 40% fat content, for 90% of my meals" – when your body lets you know that you're hungry, the RAS gets to work and highlights a healthy sandwich shop or guides you towards the healthier aisles in the supermarket.

But if you don't give the RAS specific instructions, when your body says "I'm hungry" the RAS only has a goal that's says "Feed me now", so it guides you to the first available food source and isn't choosy about what it offers. If what's nearest are sugary snacks and fast food, you then have to switch to willpower, which is a far tougher place to achieve your goals from.

It's a bit like the computer adage "Garbage in, garbage out" – if you don't program your mind for specifically what you want to find and achieve, you may well gravitate to more of what you don't want or need. So set your goals carefully.

EXERCISE 33
GET SMART

If you're like me and have had SMART drummed into your head throughout your working life, I apologise. However, only now that I understand the science of RAS do I understand why this painstaking process is actually what makes the difference between just setting goals and setting and *achieving* goals.

I'd like to help you get the best possible assistance from your RAS. This will require you to invest some time in becoming very specific about your goals. For each of the goals you have identified, complete the following:

MY GOAL IS:

Specific:
What is it that I specifically want to achieve?

What does accomplishing this goal look, sound or feel like?

Measurable/Motivational
How will I know when I've achieved it (dates, times, frequency?)

Major or minor measurable milestones to achieving it:

What will achieving this goal do for me/give me?

What will it cost me if I don't achieve it or at least have a go?

Achievable
How do I know that I can achieve this?

What could get in the way?

Resources/Requests
What resources do I need (time, money, support, personal courage etc.)?

Whose support do I need?

Describe the requests I will need to make of others whose support I will need:

Time
When specifically do I want to start and finish this goal?

What are the timings of the major milestones?

ARE YOU CREATING A STORY IN YOUR GOALS?

I have talked a great deal about the impact stories can have when trying to reach your potential. They also have a massive part to play in you not achieving your goals.

Just holding on to one limiting story around your ability to achieve your goal might well be enough to resign it to the wastepaper bin. For example, if you had set yourself the goal of running a 10k race in six months' time but you had any one of the following stories circling in your head, your chances of success would be very slim:

> *My partner will never support me and look after the children when I need to train.*
> *There's never enough time to train.*
> *I can't afford to buy a running machine for the home.*
> *I'm too old, stiff, bad at sport to do it.*

Going back to the Byron Katie process of questioning your reality can be essential in goal setting. Let me explain what I mean by looking at Jasmine's journey through her goal-setting story:

Jasmine's goal is to get fit and to run a 10k race in six months' time without feeling like she's dying. Her limiting story is: "I never have enough time for exercise."

GILL: Do you know that's true?

JASMINE: Yes, I'm totally overwhelmed with kids, job, supporting my husband, demanding relatives.

GILL: Can you be 100% sure it's true?

JASMINE: Well, if I'm honest I take on way too much of other people's problems and by the end of the day I usually end up on the couch watching the TV for a couple of hours, or catching

225

up on my or my team's work, so I guess I could find time if I asked my partner to watch the kids, stop rescuing others at work, and I could cut down on the telly a couple of nights a week.

GILL: When you tell yourself the story "I never have enough time for exercise", how do you react?

JASMINE: Oh, I just tell myself that fitting in exercise is impossible, and that it's not my fault. If I'm honest, there's a part of me that likes this story as I don't even have to consider exercising, which because I'm so unfit sounds exhausting and painful.

GILL: So do you have a story about running and exercising?

JASMINE: I guess so. I think in reality that it can be painful and a bit boring to start, but afterwards I always feel great!

GILL: Do you know that's true?

JASMINE: Well, yes and no really. I tried to kick off a running pro-gramme last year and when I did run I got hugely out of breath and really ached the next day, but if I'm being truthful here, I didn't follow the programme which advised me to build up slowly. I wanted results fast and did just about the opposite of what the programme said.

GILL: So if you could get some support, stop disempowering your team and taking on their work, reduce the TV watching and follow the programme, you might be able to find the time and over a while begin to enjoy it.

JASMINE: Maybe...?

Notice here that Jasmine is still only at the point of saying "Maybe". She has done a great job of undermining and splinter-ing her previous limiting story, but she has not yet written the new story and, even more importantly, found positive evidence to reinforce it.

GILL: Jasmine, around making enough time, what could be an alternative empowering story?

JASMINE: What, like "I have lots of time"?

226

GILL: Not quite, I think you have to be very careful to tell yourself something that is believable and realistic for you. For instance, is this goal really important to you?

JASMINE: Oh yes, I really want my fitness back. I used to be very sporty at school, and I want that feeling of looking good in my clothes and having lots of energy for my kids, who are 4 and 7.

GILL: So what about believing something like: "My fitness is incredibly important to me and therefore I will make time and get the support I need"?

JASMINE: I like the first bit, but I'm a bit nervous of the second part – you know, asking for support.

GILL: What's your story about asking for support?

JASMINE: My husband works really hard for the family and it wouldn't be fair to ask him to do more.

GILL: Do you really know that's true?

JASMINE: Hmmm, this is hard. I know it's not completely true because he does get time for his hobby and he often asks if he can help, and I work really hard too, it's just that I feel like this is my responsibility.

GILL: When you run the story that you can't ask for support, how do you feel?

JASMINE: Overwhelmed and a bit resentful.

GILL: A bit resentful?

JASMINE: OK, OK, quite a lot resentful, because he gets to do his personal stuff and I don't.

GILL: What would happen if you asked for support?

JASMINE: He'd probably say yes.

GILL: So what might be a more empowering story to tell around getting support?

JASMINE: "My needs for personal time are just as important as others in the family so I will ask for support."

GILL: That's fantastic! You may even want to add in something like "and the reason I look after my needs is that when I look after me, I'm better able and willing to look after others".

Again, it's important to state that these new stories or beliefs are only the starting point of change. You still need to build real-life evidence of positive change and movement towards your goal, but this work is a crucial first step.

EXERCISE 34
WHAT DO I DO TODAY?

The way I find most useful to begin achieving your goals is to jump ahead in time and live your life once your goal has been achieved, and then describe how you got there.

How do you live day to day or week to week? What tasks have you completed?

Then for each of your three goals set a daily or weekly achievement list.

Opposite is an example, and there's a blank for you to use on page 230.

When you have completed this for all three goals, well done!

I realise that you may feel slightly overwhelmed, and it can look like a massive undertaking when it is all written in front of you. However, you're far better to have many specific tasks to follow than none at all. If you think of your current to-do list and how many of those tasks don't sit within your values, aspirations and goals, what you are actu-

	Daily I will	Weekly I will	Monthly/quarterly I will
Goal 1			
To be able to have energy and enthusiasm to play, exercise and enjoy fresh air with my children and their children to come	Be mindful about the food choices I make	Ensure I have exercised to increase my cardiac output three times a week	Look into new exercise classes, friends to exercise with, or events to aim for in line with my fitness goals
Goal 2			
To have enough money coming in and saved to allow me to be free from worry about covering my bills	Monitor my spending choices and remain mindful of my budget for the week	Calculate, set and stick to a budget based on what I know is coming in and how much is being saved or going out	Meet with my financial adviser or seek financial advice about how to maximise my finances in line with my goals Seek opportunities to bring more money into the household finances

ally doing is prioritising, managing your time appropriately in line with who you want to be and all you wish to achieve.

Display your daily goals in a place where you can see them. A kitchen noticeboard works for me.

LOVE YOU MUM

	Daily I will	Weekly I will	Monthly/quarterly I will
Goal 1			
Goal 2			
Goal 3			

The tragedy of life does not lie in not reaching your goals, the tragedy lies in not having any goals to reach. It isn't a calamity to die with dreams unfulfilled, but it is a calamity not to dream. **—Dr Benjamin Mays**

MINDSET IN A MINUTE
LEARNING RESPONSE-ABILITY

Reflect on how you feel about the fact that your life now is not the result of your genes, parents, kids, education, job, luck, timing, health, environment, horrendous events, disability, bullying or any other factor you may want to blame. It is the choices you have made and the actions you have taken because of or in spite of the above that have brought you to where you are today.

Remember that whatever is happening in our lives, or our children's lives, we always have the power to choose how we respond to any situation. We can stop life happening to us by taking *response-ability* for the choices we make.

Don't carry baggage from a stressful event around with you for longer than you have to. Clarify, acknowledge and undertake any actions that you need to and move on. Face each new event in your day, your life in its own entirety. Keep pain from a past interaction out of the next one.

Practise circuit-breaking your automatic reactions to stressful events, utilise FAB and start responding in a way you can be comfortable with, rather than regret.

Start to take responsibility for making clear requests for what you need or want. First work out what it is, why you are frustrated, snappy or angry with those around you and choose whether a request needs to be made. If it does, make it clearly and comprehensively, not making any assumptions about what others "should" know!

When in a stalemate conversation or argument with someone, try asking why what they are wanting is important to them. Ask yourself too. Then step out of the impasse and look for how both of your interests could be met.

Re-examine your view of you as a mum in the light of your journey in this book. Know what you want to carry forward from your journey, your childhood and your experiences so far and the way you have been parenting up until now and what you definitely do not want to continue to do.

Set yourself some future goals. Use all the supporting guidance in this chapter's interlude and set that first point of achievement on the journey that is the rest of your life.

CHAPTER 6

BUILDING HABITS

When you reach the end of your life, do you want to be of the people who are glad they did, or one of the people who wish they had?

The final element of A TRUTH is building habits to take you towards your goals.

There is an abundance of evidence on the importance of creating habits in order to achieve success. The bottom line is this: you have to repeat an action enough times until it becomes a behaviour which you perform automatically, or without conscious thought. The repetition creates a mental association between the situation (cue) and action (behaviour), which means that when you encounter the cue you perform the behaviour automatically.

There's some disagreement about how long it takes to form a habit – the longstanding view is that it takes 21–28 days, although the UK Health Behaviour Research Centre has recently published research showing that it takes 66 days of repeating an action to form a habit. Think about it: if you can do something for 66 days straight, surely you can do it for a year, five years or for ever?

GAIN THE SLIGHT EDGE

There is a theory of success called the slight edge that I find seals my commitment to my daily goals.

Take a look at the graph overleaf.

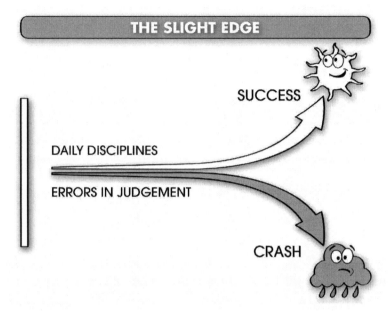

THE SLIGHT EDGE

SUCCESS

DAILY DISCIPLINES

ERRORS IN JUDGEMENT

CRASH

The two arrows on the graph begin with the same potential for success.

- ♡ The top line is a person who for a higher percentage of time makes a choice in line with their goals and vision.
- ♡ The lower line is the path of a person who daily, weekly or monthly makes a choice that isn't in line with their goals.

Look at where each of them ends up.

Take the example of two mums who have been thinking about getting some quality time with their partners to rekindle the romance and closeness. This week, both mums have the possibility of talking to their partners and organising something special.

One mum, Sue, chose to stay on the top line, and put a little time into coming up with a couple of options, discussed them and agreed a fun date with her partner.

236

The other mum, Tessa, let the opportunity slip, which is easy to do when there are so many jobs and distractions, and actually saw it as her partner's responsibility to come up with ideas for quality time as much as it was hers.

At the end of the week there is no real perceivable difference in the levels of closeness or romance of the two couples. The top-line couple did spend some fun time together, but not so much that it would make a huge difference if compared to the other couple.

But if the same decisions continue to be made for 3, then 6, then 12 months, would you begin to see a significant difference in the quality of the relationships?

Sue and her partner are able to raise sensitive issues and there's been enough trust built between them to see the love and good intentions of each partner even if the conversation gets heated.

Tessa and her partner, on the other hand, are struggling to remember why they like each other and when there is the slightest cross word, the worst picture is painted, jokes get taken the wrong way and they both begin to tiptoe round each other as if on eggshells.

Two years later, those weekly choices may have led one couple to a life of constant conflict or separation.

What is crucial about the slight edge is that it highlights that by not staying focused on the things that matter most, like health, relationships or personal down time, those areas begin to suffer. However, because the errors in judgement are daily or weekly, we don't see the damage occurring until it's too late.

Make sure that you keep the slight edge in following your goals.

STOP LYING TO YOURSELF

Quite rightly, most human beings don't particularly enjoy pain and I don't know anyone who enjoys emotional pain. This presents the human psyche with a terrible dilemma when your thoughts, decisions or actions are in conflict with your values, beliefs and goals.

You say you want something and then you do the opposite to what you say you want. Why does this happen?

There is a phenomenon in psychology known as cognitive dissonance. Unfortunately, it's a sneaky type of thinking that encourages you to make excuses. If you don't nip it in the bud, it can be deadly for your life plans and your goals.

Have you have ever been on a diet and trying your best to stay off high-calorie snacks? You then have the day from hell and the kids have left the chocolate cake out on the kitchen table. You know that you've committed to cutting right back on this type of food, but you just can't help yourself and 60 seconds later you've devoured a huge piece.

Yep, me too!

This is where the cognitive dissonance kicks in. You begin to have feelings of guilt, maybe even shame that you've let yourself down. These feelings and your actions are very uncomfortable as they don't fit the picture of how you want to see yourself, so you begin to justify your actions:

♡ "It was only one piece of cake."
♡ "I've been so good."
♡ "It's about time I did something nice for me."
♡ "It's a stupid diet anyway; I don't know why I bother."

Please don't get me wrong here; I'm not trying to preach sainthood. I have made and will continue to make decisions

238

and act in ways that are not always aligned to my values or what I'm trying to achieve.

What I am saying again is:

Be honest with yourself.... go on, really, only accept the truth.

When we lie to ourselves we slowly erode our ability to take responsibility. It's a kind of truth decay which initially makes us feel better, as we don't have to take responsibility for our choices, but slowly turns us into helpless victims as we start to blame our behaviour and decisions on our bad day at work, bad day at home, family, money troubles, busy lives, even our star sign.

I don't achieve my goals every day – just ask my friends and family. You could say I spent the first 40 years of my life failing and I will hopefully spend the next 40 or so failing too. I teach all of these concepts and still often snap, grumble, feel low, get fed up, do things that are not in line with my goals and feel bad about letting myself or others down. I aim every day to be the kind of mum I want to be alongside the woman I want to be, and of course I don't always achieve it.

What I do know absolutely is that I will try again, and keep trying, through every step, every life event, every fall. I accept that for me that is enough. I am not afraid of failing for the rest of my life as failing got me to where I am now, to the me I am now, and she is OK for me.

If you have a day when you don't do something that you know you should, just admit to yourself and learn from it. It doesn't feel good when you feel you have fallen off your chosen path, but by understanding and accepting why you have, there's a much higher likelihood that you will do something about it.

But do make sure that you haven't set yourself up to fail. For all of the goals you've set, ask yourself:

- ♡ Are they truly in line with my values and my dreams?
- ♡ Do I have an inner belief or inner voice questioning the validity of those goals?
- ♡ Are they based in the realms of possibility and are they achievable?
- ♡ Have I engaged the useful elements of RAS to help me keep my dream alive?

A troubled mother took her daughter to see Mohandas Gandhi, who was world renowned for his great spiritual discipline. It seems the young girl had become addicted to eating sweets, and her mother wanted Gandhi to speak to her about this harmful habit and convince her to drop it.

On hearing this request, Gandhi paused in silence and then told the mother, "Bring the girl back to me in three weeks and I will speak to her then."

Just as she was instructed, the mother returned with her daughter, and Gandhi, as he had promised, spoke to the girl about the detrimental effects of eating too many sweets. He counselled her to give them up.

The mother gratefully thanked Gandhi, but was perplexed. "Why," she asked him, "did you not speak to my daughter when we first came to you?"

"My good woman," Gandhi replied, "three weeks ago I myself was still addicted to sweets!"

FAILURE IS AN OPPORTUNITY TO LEARN

If inter-fear-ances are preventing you from achieving your potential and the results you want, what you may be feeling is fear. It could be false evidence appearing real or it could be stemming from a story. Your inner voice is telling you:

You're afraid of failing, letting yourself down, disappointing yourself again.

Well, the alternative is this:

You don't try, and you definitely fail!

Does that feel better?

You already know that it's all too common to really want something but never even try to go after it. If you do that, you have to accept that nothing's going to change.

Before you accept that as inevitable, let's look again at what it means to fail. Let me share with you an essential tool that I have used for many years and now share with my sons, on what seems like an hourly basis.

SUCCESS   LEARN   CHANGE

The vast majority of goals will require you to leave your comfort zone. I talked at length about comfort zones in Chapter 4. Remember, leaving your comfort zone does not have to mean experiencing unbearable pain, but it will mean:

- ♡ Not being comfortable.
- ♡ A period of uncertainty where the results you want may not be obvious.
- ♡ Moments where you fail, flounder, get rejected.

MAXIMISING YOUR LEARNING

Even though there are eventual benefits, many people who go out of their comfort zone quickly zoom back to the known and familiar if their experience isn't a pleasant one. It's worth reminding yourself of the powerful model we covered earlier, $E+S+R=O$.

Let's revisit Jasmine and her goal to get fit. Jasmine has planned to go running on Saturday morning. She's got the support of her husband and she has 90 minutes to run, stretch and shower.

Saturday morning dawns. Their daughter can't find her tennis kit and Jasmine's husband Bob, who as yet hasn't got the hang of the Saturday morning routine, is in danger of being late dropping both kids off to their sporting clubs. Jasmine feels duty bound to dive in and give a bit of support.

By the time Bob is back on track, Jasmine only has 60 minutes left before she has promised to go shopping with her mum, who has already set off from her home 40 miles away. Jasmine throws on her kit, clearly does not do anything like enough stretching and, having finally found her running shoes, actually gets about 35 minutes of the hour she was hoping for.

On her return, she manages to shower in about 2 minutes but is already starting to ache as she really didn't warm up or cool down properly. Her mum arrives as Jasmine is still wrapped in a towel and gives her a rolling-eyes-to-the-sky look to say "Jasmine's never on time".

If Jasmine's not careful she could look on her first attempt at exercise as a bit of disaster (a negative Event). It turned out to be painful, she still had to put others' needs in front of her own and she didn't really have enough time. This is a pivotal moment where the old programming could have shouted loudly "told you so" (Story). From there she could have gone into a highly negative Reaction: "What's the point, I always get dragged back to look

242

after the kids." And the Outcome? It's better to avoid future disappointment and frustration by dropping this stupid exercise goal.

Fortunately, Jasmine has been inoculated against this negativity with a new, more useful and empowering set of beliefs called Success Learn Change, or SLC for short.

You apply SLC every time you go outside your comfort zone and especially when things become challenging or you're uncertain whether you're making progress. It works by asking three questions:

♡ What have been my Successes?
♡ What have I Learnt?
♡ What will I Change or do differently next time?

Later that day Jasmine reflected on the morning's challenging run, evaluating it through the lens of SLC.

Successes:
♡ Husband agreed to help and did his best
♡ I did get out and run for 35 minutes (it felt good to have that time for me)
♡ I'm proud that my exercise programme is under way

Learning:
♡ I didn't brief or prepare my hubby well enough for the first run
♡ I didn't leave myself enough extra time for a mini-crisis
♡ I got involved in solving the mini-crisis

Changes:
♡ Better preparation the night before, including knowing exactly where my kit is
♡ Being braver and letting my husband sort it out or letting the kids be late for once
♡ Avoiding arranging a must-do activity straight after my run

Instead of wallowing in a poor-little-old-me, victim story of "What's the point?", she looks for the positives (still based in reality) and acknowledges some quick wins or mini-successes that she has actually achieved. If she'd let them, these could have been overshadowed and blocked out by the old negative stories.

Secondly, she is not being unrealistically positive; she is genuinely highlighting what was not ideal.

Finally, she learns something from the experience and creates the beginning of some actions which will make her next attempt at exercise more successful.

Crucially, SLC helps Jasmine to hold on to the two new stories she is bedding into her new mum identity: "My fitness is incredibly important to me and I will make time and ask for the support I need" and "My need for personal time is important so I will ask for support".

With failure comes the opportunity to learn and grow. In other words, to fail is to learn. The point is, without failure there is no progress. When you stop failing, you stop learning. Failure is essential to success when you view it as an opportunity to learn.

♡ What will you change tomorrow?
♡ Who would you be and what would you attempt if you knew you could not fail?

Sometimes it is wise to stop doing something if it's truly not working for you, or your needs have changed so the goal has become less relevant. At the same time, think about SLC. What would happen if you simply kept learning and changing and recognising the successes, however small they might be?

Sometimes slowly, sometimes quickly, you will move towards your goal until you've achieved it. If you feel like you're getting nowhere, try visualising a year or two into the future, and see yourself having used SLC and having now achieved several goals. You are stronger and wiser for all the learning you've had and you can see the confidence you have gained, the self-belief, the knowledge that you can live with uncertainty, you can handle setbacks, you have begun to believe that you can design and create the life you deserve!

ONE LAST EXAMPLE

My final example is a mum who took a huge chunk of her precious time to read a self-development book and then wrote out a five-page goal planner, but didn't actually do any of the things she'd written down.

The first time she didn't do the first task, she experienced unpleasant feelings: guilt, anger and disappointment. This was all amplified by the new knowledge that she was solely responsible for the choices she was making. This discomfort was stemming from cognitive dissonance, so she needed to alleviate the pain. She did this by finding a justification: "Gill said I have to first accept myself good and bad, well this choice is me accepting the bad."

She passed the responsibility back to me, the author. Unfortunately, her justification using me does not affect or hurt me; the only person it affects is her.

The second day she'd had a rough night with the kids, one child full of bugs, the other whining and unhappy, and she once again chose to not start on her goals. The dissonance was greater now, so she needed a bigger, better justification: "I'm too tired, no one could survive on four hours' sleep, I'll start tomorrow when I've had a better night."

245

Each day you choose to follow the, often very real, justifications for not moving forward is one day closer to your life flowing past you and you staying right where you are now.

Only you can choose how you respond.

Look again at each of your daily habits. Are they truly harder than how you live currently every day – or are they just different?

**Different and new will bring you just that –
a different and new you!**

Accept who you are today as you move goal by goal, choice by choice, towards the person you want to be.

FINDING YOUR SUPPORT NETWORK

My final recommendation for achieving your goals is only to share them with people who support you and really want you to become everything you could be and deserve to be.

Be very wary of sharing your goals with those who might rain on your parade. Your ambition may only heighten their own lack of self-worth and blame mentality and before you know it, they'll be attempting covertly or even overtly to tell you that you've got no chance!

Sometimes these doomsayers are the ones closest to us, including our mother, father, partner, even our teenagers. Be especially aware of your parents: if you still feel that you are the child and they are all-knowing, a word of doubt from them may knock you horribly.

You are not alone – an old cliché but in this case a true one.

In sharing A TRUTH, writing this book and running the seminars, I have seen a mass of support through my website, www.theonlymum.com. It is full of other mums who are on this journey with us.

On there you will see other mums sharing their fears and experiences, their judgements and pain, their joys, successes and dreams. It also lists the seminars and courses I run and all the other resources available to you.

When your day, your week or your journey feels tough, log on and find one of us online. I often take part in webinars and chats online, and if you need my help, I may be busy with my two boys, but I will endeavour to answer as soon as I can.

Alternatively, phone one of your friends or family members, share your journey, your fears, your judgements, your dissonance and let them hold you through the tough times.

We are all sharing the journey of giving ourselves, our children and those we love a chance of a life where joy outweighs pain, laughter supersedes tears and our reality brings us peace. Never feel you are doing it alone.

> *The greatest gift you will ever receive is the gift of loving and believing in yourself. Guard this gift with your life. It is the only thing that will ever truly be yours.* **—Tiffany Loren Rowe**

MINDSET IN A MINUTE
BUILDING HABITS

Learn from the slight edge model that each single time you make a choice that is not in line with your goals and your values you may not see a great difference in your outcome, but that over a month, a year or a lifetime, those single choices add up to you being a long way from where you hoped you would be.

Understand that your mind and cognitive dissonance will create what feels like totally acceptable and justifiable excuses for every step you take away from your goals. Use your new aware-ness to clarify if you have created an excuse story and start breaking through to your truth.

Keep your awareness of A TRUTH in your mind. Challenge your-self as to whether you are truly being honest with yourself.
     Only you know – why lie to yourself any longer?

Remember that if you never try to achieve any of the things you want in your life, you will definitely guarantee to fail.

Identify what success you can glean from each hurdle you fall at, what you can learn from it and what you will do differently next time.

     Success   Learn   Change

Your different actions, your different ways of choosing response-ability will bring you a different you and peace with yourself, the you you have always been and will always be.

249

LOVE YOU MUM

Find the rest of us on our journeys and be part of the support of motherhood on www.theonlymum.com.

CHAPTER 7

PARENTING WITH A TRUTH

I promised that this book isn't a parenting book, it's a book for mums. However, when I talk to mums day in and day out in the course of my work, I get asked all the time how these techniques can help us to make the right parenting choices and how to make a difference in the way we respond to our kids. In this final chapter I'm going to demonstrate how you can apply A TRUTH in a practical way and also some rescue remedies.

This is a whistle-stop tour as I don't want to move the focus away from you. Should you want far more detail and further examples, please look on my website, www.theonly-mum.com.

By the sheer fact that you are reading a book on being a mum, I can deduce that you do not operate in a quiet, calm, adult-only zone but the usual challenging, fun-filled, chaotic place that is called family life.

How I choose to parent and my opinions on parenting are based on the values that my husband and I hold, our chosen path, and our individual children and how they grow within our family. Our choices of the methods we use to help our children eat, sleep, learn about society's rules, their education, their emotions and their health work for us, but would not necessarily work for either you or your children. I am by no means an expert on parenting and would never profess to be.

What I can share with you is the elements of this book that are particularly useful when some of the parenting obstacles seem tough, and when the inter-fear-ance that you are experiencing is coming directly from your children or your beliefs about your children's behaviour. I can also share how you can utilise the mindset technique FAB when handling parenting choices moment by moment, and when you quite simply cannot.

AWARE

You may have entered into parenting having read books, taken courses, spoken to others about the entire spectrum of parenting wisdom, from Gina Ford and Ferberizing to attachment or continuum parenting and any of the advice in between. Or you may have read nothing and make instant or considered choices at each stage of your child's development.

However you sit on that spectrum, one thing is for sure: if you and your partner are not aware of what you both consider good parenting to look like, what hopes, dreams and visions you hold for your children's upbringing, you have a recipe for an interesting parenting experience.

I have heard more stories of frustration, tantrums, anger and tears (and that's just the parents) when two parents disagree, contradict each other, allow different standards, work separately or just never discuss their needs when bringing up their children. Two people with totally different stories, sets of values, thoughts, feelings and needs attempting to face the joyful challenge that children bring is a sure-fire recipe for mayhem.

So becoming aware has two elements.

First, are you and your partner aware of each other's values and beliefs around the key areas of parenting?

Where do the children sit on the priority ladder? Are you happy that your life has become child centred? Do you accept child-based leisure time, holidays, meal times? Do you listen to your children talk before other adults, or each other? Or should the children fit into your lifestyle, your choices as adults? Should they wait until adults have stopped talking to be heard? Is life continuing as if the child had had little or no impact? Or has your life changed beyond recognition and are you both happy with that?

Do you know where you both stand on the following areas:

♡ Manners: the necessity for please and thank-you, table manners, respect for elders, saying "excuse me", "may I" and so on.
♡ Discipline: smacking, shouting at children, naughty steps and time-outs, asking your child what the problem is and really listening.
♡ Eating: whether they must empty their plate, must eat what they are given, no sugar, no sweets, baby-led weaning, child choosing and helping to make their food.
♡ Sleeping: set routine at bedtime, crying it out, staying in own bed, daytime naps, letting them stay up until they fall asleep or ask for bed.
♡ Developing and learning: enforcing homework, sharing homework or ignoring homework, extra tuition, exam and result focus, child-centred learning, home schooling.
♡ Freedom as they grow: age-relevant boundaries, walking to school alone, no longer needing childcare, setting curfews, alcohol, smoking, drugs, sex, partners sleeping in your house, freedom to explore growing up, further education, career.

We face all of these and many more choices as parents. But often the reality is that we face them in the moment as a child leaps into a new stratosphere of development and bounds into the next challenge. Potty training, tantrums, friends, hobbies, school subject choices, sex... do you think about these in advance or when they happen?

You also need an emergency plan when one parent encounters a new challenge so that they feel safe in the knowledge that they are supported in their actions. This comes from knowing each other's values, each other's beliefs on behaviour and what boundaries you both place on discipline and expectations.

One thing remains true for all the stages we face as parents: how you respond in those critical new experiences with your child is absolutely crucial. It is the way your child remembers what you stood for, who you were and how you treated them when things got tough.

Secondly, become aware of both your own and your child's voice.

Listen to yourself

You have spent the last 250 or so pages learning to listen to your inner voice and your intuition. This is the most critical and essential parenting tool I can share with you.

Whatever your beliefs about the right of children to choose, there will always be occasions when for either safety or necessity you have to make choices for your children. In the first few years you make practically every decision for them.

This is where hearing your inner voice and your intuition is essential. In the midst of the noise and madness around you day to day, find time to take a couple of deep breaths and check that you are on track with the choices you are making.

You already know that your inner voice can be working from a story, a thought created by what you believe things should be. Analyse and assess whether you are hearing your pure inner voice, or whether you are climbing your ladder, thinking from a story, or if an inter-fear-ance is getting in the way of your clarity.

Read books, talk to friends, talk to your partner and then choose your parenting route. Do not allow others' opinions to sway you, unless your intuition thinks that their solution is a useful one for you. Remember the power of PLOMing, the pity party, the judgements and assumptions that people and you can make. Turn off all the noise, don't let guilt or doubt cloud your mind, listen to what you know is right and stick with it jointly and consistently, knowing that your intention is to make the best choices for your child.

For example, if you have chosen never to let your baby cry it out at bedtime, be OK with that. You made that choice for your own intuitive reasons. At times it will be tough, tiring, frustrating, demoralising, but the first time your child soothes him- or herself calmly to sleep you will know that every second of the journey was worth it.

It may be very hard to hear how much more quickly other methods work and that other people's children are contented and well rested sooner than yours. Know what works for you and hold to it.

Listen to your child
From incredibly early on in life, a child learns to find ways to communicate their needs or attempt to. From day one they have different cries for different needs and they very quickly discover their own ways of trying to get their message across to you. But against the constant noise of mummyhood, we can't always hear what our children are trying to say.

What is essential for finding your awareness is a stop gap. Breathing in deeply to a count of 6 and then out for 6 is an instant life silencer, to get you to stop and listen.

If your child is not talking yet, either watch for their non-verbal signs – a hand to the mouth for hunger, rubbing their eyes when tired – or tune into their connection to your intuition. You will often sense what your child needs and just a little silence can help you hear it.

As your children start to communicate even in those tentative stages of verbal command, get into the habit of asking them what they need. Trust your child's instinct about their own needs (how often have you seen your child stop eating a food they adore, because they are quite simply full?) – they are often more in touch with themselves than many of us! They can tell you loud and clear what they believe they need. I don't advocate that you always deliver the requested six-flavour ice cream or trip to the moon that they desire, but you can make the choice with them or alone as to whether that need can be met. What you are doing for your child is both cultivating their own trust in themselves and identifying their needs, but also some autonomy in being part of a decision too.

Even when they're tantruming, hysterical or stroppy, a calm, centred parent asking them what they need, or even using their intuition to guess for them, can have an amazing effect. It doesn't work every time but it does work sometimes.

For example, you need to leave the playground and go home for tea. Just as you really do need to get going, your 3 year old lies down on the floor and refuses to move. Once you've allowed him to vent his feelings for as long as you have time for, take your deep breaths and say: "Are you really enjoying being at the park? Are you feeling sad and angry that it is time to go home?" Repeat this a couple of times if you need to, but just as our own feelings dissipate when they've been aired and acknowledged, so do a child's.

Try it on a child of any age. Acknowledge the feelings you believe they are strongly and loudly experiencing and

256

state, without a solution or change of plan, what you believe they must be thinking. Show them that you empathise; you do need to actually find empathy for them, not just annoyance, for your words to have congruence. Listen to their feelings and see their pain dissipate. Try it and let me know how it works for you!

THOUGHTS, REALITY AND UNDERSTANDING

We can never parent in isolation – we are surrounded by media, society, friends and family members who have thoughts, opinions and advice on what our children should be like. They are bound to influence us, just as we have a story about what a good mum should be like.

Consciously or not, from the moment you saw that blue line on the pregnancy test you started forming a story about what your child should, could or would be like. Even the most aware of parents have unwittingly painted this picture.

As your children grow and develop you still carry that picture with you, now often buried deep in the imagination of pregnancy but still very much alive and vivid. Combined with the odd overheard comment, the look from the other mums at nursery, the feedback on the school report, you start to measure your child against imaginary expectations. Those expectations are an amalgamation of stories, your ladder of inference, your childhood experiences, your unmet or unfulfilled dreams, your disappointments.

However unconscious all those thoughts, stories, feelings and needs are within you, they will leak out in your behaviour. Believe me, even if you never say a word your child will know how they are performing in your eyes.

What a platform to start life from: trying to meet a benchmark that not only does the child not know, but 9 times out of 10 the parent does not even realise is there.

Your child is unique and completely perfect, just as they are.
　　Accept the reality of them.
　　Learn to understand who they are.
　　That is the reality!

Your child is not and will never be your or anyone else's picture of what they *should* be.

TAKING RESPONSIBILITY

In my humble opinion, it is your first and foremost responsibility as a parent to get to know, befriend, love and respond to your unique child. Watch them, listen to them, support them and nurture them. Sit back and observe them, from early on let them choose the game, choose the story and have choices about their day. Leave behind the inter-fear-ance of what you wanted them to be and love them for who they are.

Through this book you have made a decision to find and reach the full potential of who you want to be. What a wonderful mindset gift to give your children: the belief and opportunity from the very start of their life that they are amazing, just being them.

Unless you home school them, wrap them in a giant bubble and never let them speak to anyone else, they will soon learn the impact of society and the noise and inter-fear-ance it can bring. Carrying a level of self-belief about being true to themselves is the best coat of armour I can imagine.

FINALLY, BUILDING PARENTING HABITS

The ability to step back and observe your unique child, to take deep breaths when they are causing you challenge, and to listen to your intuition, turning off your stories about what your child should be doing, is not only a daily discipline, it is sometimes required by the minute, even by the second.

For these actions to become your parenting habits, you have to consciously choose to do them for ever.

At each crucial step forward or backward for your child, build your emotionally intelligent parenting habits:

♡ Remain curious, using "fascinating" whenever required, allowing you to observe and learn from what your child is showing you.

♡ Stay aware of what your intuition believes is right for your child when they cannot say.

♡ Ask your child what they need and are feeling, acknowledging their pain or joy and working through with them whether their need can be met.

♡ Stay in tune with your thoughts, stories and judgements about what your child should be doing.

♡ Love, relish, accept and understand the children you have been given, for who they are in reality, not what you hoped or wanted them to be.

♡ Take responsibility to work on all of these habits and to stay aware of your inter-fear-ances as you guide your children through theirs.

♡ Love them, as them, just as you are learning to love you, as you.

Good luck my friends and goodbye, your journey with me in this book is complete...

ACKNOWLEDGEMENTS

First, a huge thank-you to all the mums who in one way or another helped me create this book: to those who worked through all the exercises, those who shared their stories to help the learning make sense, and those who have opened up about their own fears and doubts to let other mums know that they are not alone. (Don't worry, all your names have been changed!)

For the mums who read my drafts or tested the website and forum and gave me their honest feedback and support, thank you for your long hours too. Sorry the deadlines were always so tight.

For my Bumps and Babies, Blue Penguin and Westbourne Mummy Mafia mums who know better than anyone else how often I need a helping hand, a cup of coffee or a listening ear, thank you for all your cake and biscuits, friendship, support, enthusiasm and love. Oh, and the Westbourne Starbucks team, I'm going home now, I promise...

Thank you to Sally, my editor, who transformed my babble written long into the night, often with a wide-awake Jake on my lap, into something that looks coherent and readable.

Thank you to Emma, the creator of all the concepts for the cartoons, the funniest, brightest mum I know, who has no idea how brilliant she is. And to all the rest of the amazing team who helped me pull this book together, Gerry, Sarah, Helen, Al, Sue, Ian, Stuart and all the others: thank you for your patience, hard work and ideas. To all at Barnes Holland, you are an amazing team!

Thanks also to Kevin, whose experience, care, skills and wisdom helped me see that I could love *me*.

Thanks to the three ladies and all the teachers at Blue Penguin, who ensured that my boys were loved for every second I was writing this book away from them. To my mum, for every emergency dash across town to cover me, every tear mopped up and your love and support. To Julie, for being a brilliant mum two days a week when I was not there to be one. To Tina, for loving my boys as if they were your own, and from the very beginning of my journey as a mum supporting, loving and sorting me out whenever I or my fridge needed it! Thank you!

Finally, to my boys, Al, Josh, Jake and Wilson.

Josh and Jake, you two have been my greatest teachers, I feel blessed every day to have you in my life, and yes, I have finished work now!

Al, I could not have imagined sharing the adventure of becoming a mum with anyone else. Thank you for travelling beside me, challenging, supporting and believing in me, even when I didn't. Without you, none of this would have been possible, especially the making babies bit! My love, always... strength and honour!

And finally, as always Wilson, sorry you fell off the bottom of the to-do list. Yes, now I have got time to take you for a walk...